the national archaeological
museum of naples

Soprintendenza Speciale
per i Beni Archeologici di
Napoli e Pompei

# the national archaeological museum of naples

guide

**Electa**

*Front cover*
The Alexander Mosaic, from the House
of the Faun in Pompeii

p. 2
The Alexander Mosaic, detail

**Museo Archeologico Nazionale
di Napoli**
*scientific direction*
Pietro Giovanni Guzzo
Valeria Sampaolo

*texts by*
Rosanna Cappelli
Annalisa Lo Monaco

Reprint 2014
First edition 2009

www.electaweb.com

# Contents

## ground floor

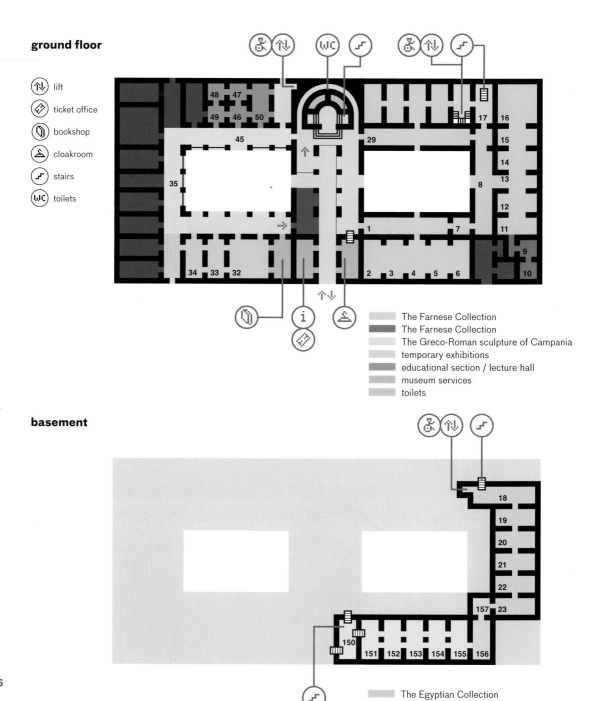

- (lift) lift
- (ticket office) ticket office
- (bookshop) bookshop
- (cloakroom) cloakroom
- (stairs) stairs
- (WC) toilets

48 47
49 46 50
45
35

29
17 16
15
14
8 13
12
1 7 11
9
34 33 32
2 3 4 5 6 10

The Farnese Collection
The Farnese Collection
The Greco-Roman sculpture of Campania
temporary exhibitions
educational section / lecture hall
museum services
toilets

## basement

18
19
20
21
22
157 23
150
151 152 153 154 155 156

The Egyptian Collection
The Epigraphic Collection

## mezzanine floor

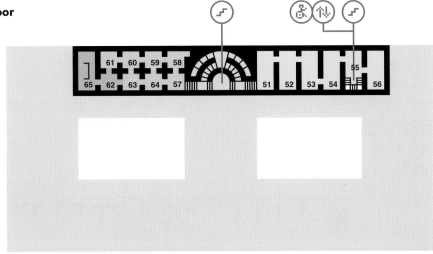

The Secret Cabinet
The Mosaic Collection
The Coin and Medal Collection

## first floor

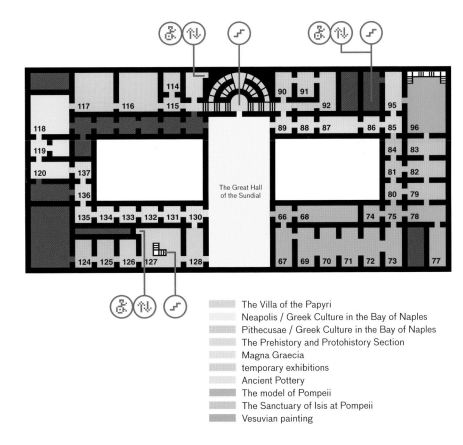

The Great Hall
of the Sundial

The Villa of the Papyri
Neapolis / Greek Culture in the Bay of Naples
Pithecusae / Greek Culture in the Bay of Naples
The Prehistory and Protohistory Section
Magna Graecia
temporary exhibitions
Ancient Pottery
The model of Pompeii
The Sanctuary of Isis at Pompeii
Vesuvian painting

7

# The history of the Museum and its collection of antiquities

To reconstruct the complicated historical events that led to the creation of the Museum, we must go back in time to the first half of the 18th century and to the enlightened cultural attitude of Charles III of Bourbon, who came to the throne of Naples in 1734. From his mother (Elizabeth Farnese), he inherited an exceptional collection of works of art and antiquities, which at that time were divided between Naples, Rome (the Palazzo Farnese, the Farnese Gardens on the Palatine Hill, the Villa Farnesina and the Villa Madama) and Parma (the Ducal Palace of Colorno). During his fifth year on the throne (1738), Charles III of Bourbon commissioned the construction of the Royal Villa of Capodimonte, which was destined to house the 'Farnese Museum'. In the same year the king instigated a particularly successful series of excavations at Resina, near one of the royal holiday residences. This area had already been investigated thirty years previously by the Prince d'Elboeuf, who had discovered the statues that subsequently were brought together in the collection of the family of Maria Amalia di Saxony, wife of Charles III. This was how the lavish sculptural decoration of the stage building of the Herculaneum theatre was discovered, a remarkable series of marble and bronze statues, with many inscriptions besides. Just ten years later, in 1748, the excavations of Pompeii began, followed a year later (1749) by those of nearby Stabiae. Amazing finds were made as a result of these excavations, bronze and marble statues (like those from the Villa of the Pisones at Herculaneum (excavated 1754-58), even exceptional discoveries like the papyri that formed the library of that villa. The huge collection of material that was found (including mosaics, items of daily life, weapons, luxury items and glass vessels, besides the superb paintings) was housed in the rooms of the Royal Villa of Portici, and formed the core of the historic *Museum Herculanense* (1750). Thanks in great part to these famous and unprecedented discoveries, Naples, already the capital of a new kingdom, also became a required stop on the Grand Tour. This was a sort of cultural pilgrimage that all the wealthy young men of Europe had to undertake to round off their education.

But the threat posed to Portici by Vesuvius (there had been more than ten eruptions in the previous century) and the slow progress being made on the Capodimonte Villa, convinced Charles III's successor, Ferdinand IV of Bourbon, to unify the family collections into one magnificent Museum. For this reason, the imposing Palazzo degli Studi of Naples was chosen "for the use of the Royal Museum of Portici, the Picture Gallery of Capodimonte, the grand Public Library, the School of the Three Fine Arts,

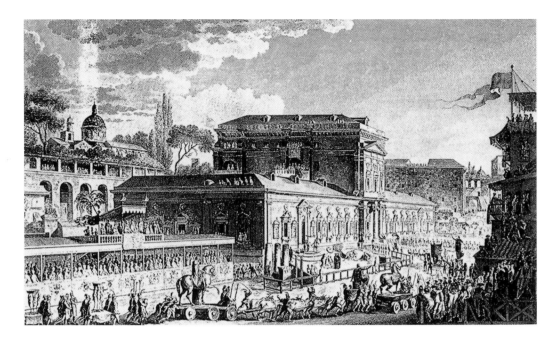

and the Room for Study of the Nude." The restructuring of this dilapidated late Renaissance building was initially assigned to the architect Ferdinando Fuga, but then passed to Pompeo Schiantarelli. It was Schiantarelli's idea to build an upper floor and the grand semi-circle at the back of the building "so that the ensemble may further beautify the capital and serve the convenience of the people" (1780). This extension of the space employed in the museum accorded well with a bold scheme, already proposed by Vanvitelli, to transfer to Naples the fabulous Farnese collection of Roman antiquities. This difficult and expensive process, begun in 1787 and continued for several years, was undertaken under the supervision of the antiquarian Domenico Venuti and the painter Philipp Hackert, acting on behalf of Ferdinand IV. It was a complicated operation. The transfer of antiquities took several years to complete, and, in some cases, it took years before particular works of art were eventually established in their final location in the museum – for example, the Farnese Bull, which only came to the museum in 1826.

The new museum project eventually abandoned the most grandiose aspects of the scheme. For example, in 1791, it was intended to add to the original plan for the Palazzo degli Studi an astronomical observatory, to be set up in the Grand Salon. In the end the only part of this completed was a Sundial that still provides the name of the room. The political upheavals of those years, during which the king fled to Palermo twice (1798 and 1806), and the decade of French rule by Joseph Bonaparte and Joachim Murat (1806-

Transportation of the antiquities
of Herculaneum from the Museum
of Portici to the Palazzo degli Studi
in Naples, from the *Voyage pittoresque
ou description des Royaumes
de Naples et de Sicile*, by the Abbé
de Saint-Non, Paris 1781-1786

Antonio Canova, Marble statue
of Ferdinand IV as Minerva

1815), did not help the completion of construction work on the new Neapolitan Museum. It was finally inaugurated in 1816 with the name 'Royal Bourbon Museum'.

The Museum's subsequent history is linked to its Directors, Michele Arditi (1810-1838), Francesco Maria Avellino (1838-1849) and Giuseppe Fiorelli (1863-1875). Fiorelli was the forerunner of the policies of conservation and sensitive exploitation of the territory that are the basis of the modern conception of a museum of antiquities.

At the turn of the 20th century the positivist historian Ettore Pais oversaw the reorganization of the Museum's collections in a manner innovative for that period, and which until recently remained essentially unchanged. Central to his scheme were contextual groupings, an emphasis on prehistory, and the strong historical accent given to particular displays (Pompeian paintings, Portraits, Greek sculpture).

Further restructuring began in 1957, and the Picture Gallery was transferred to Capodimonte. The new arrangement provides an extraordinary opportunity to reflect on the function of the Museum: to preserve the tradition and prestige of the royal collections, while at the same time linking the Museum more closely to the history and archaeology of the area.

Runners, detail. From the Villa
of the Papyri in Herculaneum

# ground floor

## Herculaneum

The new arrangement (2009) of the monumental atrium maintains its historical appearance with a selection of public statuary from Herculaneum.

The excavations of Herculaneum began in the early years of the 18th century, and achieved great intensity under the Bourbons (1738-1780). These were the years in which the most important civic buildings – the *Augusteum* (so-called Basilica), the theatre, the Basilica Noniana and the Villa of the Papyri – were excavated by means of a system of subterranean tunnels and pulleys, using soldiers and forced labour. It was only in 1828, during the reign of Frances I of Bourbon, that open-air excavations were undertaken. These lasted until 1875. Despite an enormous expenditure of labour, only *insulae* II and VII were brought to light by these excavations. The majority of the buildings that today make up the archaeological park of Herculaneum were uncovered during systematic excavations directed by A. Maiuri between 1927 and 1958. In the last twenty years the area of the ancient beach has been explored. It is here that the 12 rooms with arched entrances (the so-called *Fornici*), in which the inhabitants of the city sought shelter during the eruption, were exposed, along with the area around the Villa of the Papyri and the area by the so-called north-west *insula*.

Together, the excavations have uncovered about a quarter of the ancient city (the total area of which was about 20 hectares), as well as a small part of the suburban Villa of the Papyri. The earliest phases of urban development remain unknown at this time, because such a small part of the urban fabric has been uncovered. A profound urban renewal took place in the Augustan age; the *Macellum*, the Theatre, the Basilica, the walls, the gates, the Seat of the Augustales, a *Chalcidicum,* the aqueduct, the Central Baths, the Palaestra and possibly also the earliest manifestations of the temples of the Sacred Suburban Area all were built or underwent major restoration.

The statue of *M. Nonius Balbus*,
donated by the people of Nuceria,
from the public area of Herculaneum

## The Theatre

The theatre was constructed in the north-west part of the city in the early Augustan age. It has never been excavated to open-air, and even today can only be visited by means of 18th century tunnels. Only a few of the statues discovered can be identified securely: the famous equestrian statues of Nonius Balbus, son and father, from the portico to the side of the *frons scaenae*, and the two bronze statues of Agrippina and Antonia Minor, which, according to a recent suggestion, may have been located within the aediculae on the west and east sides of the stage. A recent hypothesis places the imperial bronze statues (Livia) and the togate statue of Tiberius in the rectangular exedra of the *summa cavea*. Bronze statues of distinguished locals, wearing togas (such as *M. Calatorius Quartio* and *L. Mammius Maximus*) were probably part of the rich architectural decoration of the *frons scaenae*.

## *Augusteum*

The structure of the so-called Basilica (today more correctly identified as the *Augusteum*) has never been the subject of systematic exploration, except during the rapid excavation campaigns of the 18th century. Thus it is very difficult to reconstruct its original sculptural and decorative programme, and in some cases even the provenance of statues from the building is still debated. The 18th century reports refer to three marble statues located on a podium, and two colossal marble statues of seated male figures with the *paludamentum* draped over their lower bodies (restored as Augustus and Claudius). In addition they mention a statue of the emperor Titus standing, crowned with a wreath, and two bronze statues, of Augustus and Claudius, depicted heroically nude. The imperial cycle is completed by statues of women, illustrated by the discovery of two bronze statues of Agrippina Minor, and a third of uncertain identity, along with several inscriptions referring to Livia and Antonia Minor. With the exception of the colossal bronze statue of Claudius, the majority of the statues that depict members of the Julio-Claudian family were donated in AD 49-50 by *L. Mammius Maximus*, at his own expense. He was a rich freedmen, a member of the college of the Augustales. His generosity was repaid with a bronze statue set up in his honour in the theatre; this is the same man who paid for work at the public market (*Macellum*), and thus it is likely that he also financed the construction of the *Augusteum*. The *Augusteum* was built during the reign of Claudius, around AD 50, and later renovated during the Flavian period. At this time images of Titus, Domitia, Julia Titia and Flavia Domitilla were added. In addition to the statues and inscriptions, other exceptional finds were made in this building, such as four large format fresco panels depicting Theseus, liberator of the young Athenians, Hercules and Telephus, Achilles and the centaur Chiron, and Pan and young Olympus. These must have adorned the two apsidal niches located symmetrically at the rear of the building.

Bronze statue of Augustus
from the *Augusteum* of Herculaneum

# ground floor

## The Farnese Collection

The Farnese Collection was the most famous of the collections of antiquities collections in Renaissance Rome. It was started by Pope Paul III Farnese, who issued an edict that gave his family the right to excavate in order to obtain marble and stone, with an exclusive claim on all sculpture, for the construction and decoration of his main residence in Rome, the Palazzo Farnese (today the French Embassy). Thus in 1545 the famous Farnese Bull was uncovered in the Baths of Caracalla, a year later the Hercules. The collection grew considerably through the efforts of the Pope's grandson, Cardinal Alessandro, one of the leading patrons of the arts of his day. During his lifetime the Farnese collection grew to more than 400 sculptures (inventoried by Domenico Venuti), besides paintings, gems, books, drawings.

This enormous collection of works of art concentrated in the Palazzo, displayed beneath the archways, in the courtyards and gardens, and, of course, inside the reception rooms. Michelangelo designed some of the settings within which some of the masterpieces were located.

Other works, considered of minor importance, were kept in the family's other Roman residences (the Villa Madama, the Villa Farnesina at Lungara and the Farnese Gardens on the Palatine Hill), in the Villa Caprarola and in the Ducal Palace of Colorno in Parma. The latter can boast possession, among other things, of two colossal basalt statues of Hercules and Dionysus excavated by Abbot Bianchini in Rome, near the Imperial Palace.

The Farnese dynasty came to an end in 1731, and its inheritance passed to the Bourbons through Elizabeth Farnese, wife of Philip V of Spain and mother of Charles, shortly to become King of Naples (1734). It was Charles who transferred the Parma collection to Naples, and his son, Ferdinand IV who asked the Pope for permission to do the same with the Roman collections. Amidst controversy, permission was eventually granted in 1787.

The statues found in the Baths of Caracalla are still today emblematic of the great value and richness of the collection. Among them, the Farnese Bull is a masterpiece of ancient art that shares with the Laocoon of the Vatican Museums the privilege of being mentioned in the *Natural History* of Pliny the Elder.

The Farnese Bull, detail

## The Farnese Bull

This colossal marble sculptural group represents the myth of the punishment of Dirce. Dirce was the wife of Lykos, king of Thebes. Her punishment was at the hands of Amphion and Zethus, the twins borne by the beautiful Antiope, who had been seduced by Zeus in the guise of a satyr. Driven out by her father Nycteus, Antiope lived in servitude with her uncle Lykos. She suffered on-going maltreatment from his wife, Dirce, who was jealous of her beauty. To avenge their mother, Amphion and Zethus tied Dirce to the horns of a bull. The bull dragged her away, tearing her body on the rocks. The sculptural group was found in fragments during the summer of 1545 in the courtyard of the Baths of Caracalla at Rome, during excavations commissioned by Pope Paul III Farnese.

Pliny records a sculpture of a similar subject, a masterpiece of Apollonius and Tauriscus of the Rhodian school, active at the end of the 2nd century BC and brought to Rome by Asinius Pollius. The Farnese Bull, one of the greatest sculptures to have come down to us from antiquity, has been interpreted variously as the original, as a copy of the Julio-Claudian period, and – more likely – as a replica of the Severan period. Reactions of artists and intellectuals to the discovery of this work of art were truly extraordinary, in many ways quite similar to the reaction a few years earlier when the Laocoon was discovered. Many described "this marvelous mountain of marble as the most singular and amazing work of the chisel of the ancient world, sculpture its most excellent form."

It was shipped to Naples in 1788, where it arrived escorted by a warship, to be placed in the garden of the Royal Villa as the central ornament of a fountain. Since 1826 it has been on permanent display in the halls of the Naples Museum.

## Farnese Hercules

This colossal statue was discovered in the mid-1500s in the Baths of Caracalla and was displayed in the courtyard of the Palazzo Farnese in Rome until 1787. From there it was moved to Naples, first to Capodimonte and then, in 1792, to the newly opened museum in the Palazzo degli Studi. During the tumultuous years of French rule, the statue escaped the designs of Napoleon, who plotted for it to be shipped to France on at least three occasions.

The statue has been restored on numerous occasions, most famously by Guglielmo della Porta who was commissioned by Michelangelo to remake its lost legs. When the original legs were found the Farnese family chose not to replace them, 'to demonstrate that works of modern sculpture can stand comparison with ancient works'. It was only later that the Bourbons reinserted the original legs, after the king of Naples received them as a gift from the Borghese family.

The inscription carved on the rock beneath the club attributes the work to the Athenian sculptor Glykon. The statue is a copy of the colossal bronze of 'Hercules at Rest' by Lysippus of Sicyon.

## Ephesian Artemis

The sanctuary of Artemis at Ephesis was one of the most important sanctuaries of the Greco-Eastern work, and enjoyed great prosperity and fame even into the Roman imperial period. The cult image of the goddess, of which countless replicas of every conceivable form and material exist, is only known to us from the Hellenistic age, from images on coins minted at Ephesus. The goddess' head is covered by a *kalathos,* sometimes in the shape of a temple, behind which a veil forms a kind of circular nimbus decorated with griffin protomes. Her dress is richly decorated: on her chest a necklace, adorned with ribbons and *pendants*, beneath which are rows of breasts (or the scrota of bulls which had been sacrificed) symbolizing fertility; on the lower part of her body is a neat sequence of animal protomes, sphinxes, bees, flowers, and nymphs. Her arms, stretched before her, would have held a ribbon. The example from the Farnese Collection is a copy made in alabaster during the imperial period. The bronze parts of the statue relate to a restoration by Giuseppe Valadier.

## The Carracci Gallery

This was the name of one of the most famous rooms in the Palazzo Farnese in Rome. It was built by Cardinal Odoardo, and the frescoes were painted by the Bolognese artist Annibale Carracci at the end of the 16th century. The Gallery was designed with ten niches and six *tondi,* and housed ancient statues and busts. The statues, now divided between the Naples Museum and the British Museum in London, included sculptures of such works as Dionysus, Eros, Apollo, Hermes, and Antinous, the one statue of Ceres and sculptural groups representing Ganymede embracing Zeus' eagle, and a Satyr with Dionysus as a child.
The busts of several Roman emperors were also displayed in the Gallery with these statues. They formed just a small part of the exceptional set of imperial portraits and herms of Greek intellectuals and philosophers originally displayed in the Great Hall of the Emperors in the Palazzo Farnese. Their arrangement in the Naples Museum, in the two Halls of Greek and Roman portraits, is a deliberate attempt to copy the original display, to record the antiquarian ethos of the period.

## Farnese Caracalla

This bust of the emperor Caracalla is recorded in the 1568 inventory of the Farnese Collection. It adorned the family's Roman palace until it was transferred to Naples in 1796 (first to Capodimonte, then to the Palazzo degli Studi). Its fame during the 17th and 18th centuries owes much to the Roman emperor's bad reputation, caused by his violent temper and his crime of fratricide. Winckelmann wrote that even Lysippus could not have made a better portrait. A bronze copy was commissioned by Pope Pius IV from Guglielmo della Porta, for his Vatican Belvedere collection; it later became part of the Roman Farnese collection and today is housed in the Capodimonte Museum.

## Bust of Homer

The facial features of the greatest Greek poet have been reproduced since classical times, starting a tradition that continued until the fall of the Roman empire.

Thus this is a 'reconstructed' portrait. The artist strove to project in the portrait what tradition had for centuries built up around the mythical figure of the bard. The distinctive elements of his portrait were his blindness and old age, the first being an almost essential condition for the memory, the second a natural condition of one who aspires to be a scholar and intellectual. The portrait-type of Homer was one of the most popular of the Classical period, displayed in sanctuaries and libraries, such as the celebrated *Homereion* of Alexandria, a centre for Homeric studies in the Hellenistic age. In the words of Christodorus, when he saw the poet's statue at the Baths of Constantinople: "... the features of an old man, but of a gentle old age, so much so that it gives him an even richer aura of grace: a mix of venerability and admiration, from which prestige shines through ... With his two hands supported by his staff, one on top of the other, like a real man. The right ear bent, as if always listening to Apollo, almost as if he could hear a Muse nearby ..." (*Anthologia Palatina,* II, 311-349). The portrait in the Farnese collection is a Hellenistic type of the 2nd century BC, widely known from many replicas and probably a creation of the Rhodian School.

25

## The Tyrannicides

In 514 BC two young Athenians, Harmonius and Aristogeiton, killed Hipparchos, the younger son of the tyrant Pisistratus, and paid for the act with their lives. The Athenian democratic party later made their gesture the symbol of liberty itself and, as soon as the Tyrants were banished (510 BC), two bronze statues of the two heroes, made by the sculptor Antenor, were set up in the Agora. When the Persians occupied the city in 480 BC, they took the statues as spoils and carried them back to Susa. They were given back to the Athenians by the successors of Alexander the Great a century and a half later. After their victory over the Persians, the Athenians decreed that a new bronze statue group should be erected, and entrusted its execution to *Kritios* and *Nesiotes* (477 BC). Images of this group, by then a symbol of patriotism and of the cult of ancient Attic virtues, survive on coins, painted vases and reliefs. On the basis of these reproductions it has been possible to identify these two statues in Naples, Roman copies of the 2nd century BC, found at Hadrian's Villa in Tivoli. The figures are an example of the 'severe style' at its height. The bodies are wiry and powerful, but devoid of the archaic calligraphisms still found, for example, on the pediments of Aegina. Both figures are portrayed in action: Harmodius, the beardless young man, is attacking with his arm raised, while Aristogeiton stretches his arm forward to shield his friend. Aristogeiton's head is a cast of a head from the Vatican. A splendid ancient copy of the bronze original was found in Baiae and is on display in the Museo dei Campi Flegrei at Baia Castle. This sculptural group was already famous in antiquity for having introduced the fashion for 'iconic' statues, previously unknown in Greece. As Pliny notes, "it was the custom to depict the likeness only of those individuals who deserved immortality for some illustrious reason; at first for the victories achieved at the sacred games, more particularly at the Olympic Games, where it was common practice to dedicate a statue to all the victors. And if anyone won three times, his statue was made with the exact likeness of each limb; for this reason they were called 'iconic'. I do not know if the Athenians were the first to erect statues at public expense, in honour of the Tyrannicides Harmodius and Aristogeiton... This custom was later adopted by the whole world." (*Natural History*, 34, 9-10)

## Venus Kallipygia

This statue was discovered in the course of excavations at the *Domus Aurea* in Rome. It depicts the goddess about to bathe, turning her head to admire her own body reflected in the water. The genre of the nude female figure, depicted with an almost "rococo" taste typical of the Hellenistic period, became a familiar one after the creation of the Aphrodite of Cnidos, Praxiteles' masterpiece. Such works were often employed in the decorative schemes of fountains. The name *Kallipygia* (literally "with beautiful buttocks") was attributed to this statue in error, with reference to a famous work of art known to have been on display in a temple at Syracuse in the 2nd century BC. This statue must have been a famous one, as is clear by comparison with its many replicas, depicted on gems and as bronze statuettes. After its rediscovery, it was clumsily restored by Albacini, who was responsible for the head, the shoulders, the left arm and drapery, the right hand and right calf.

# ground floor

## The gems of the Farnese Collection

The passion for ancient gems became a noteworthy cultural phenomenon in the Renaissance. One of the largest collections, later incorporated into the Farnese corpus, was the 'Barbo', put together by Pietro Barbo, later Pope Paul II (1464). He was an enthusiastic collector, and his collection was based in the Palazzo San Marco (the Palazzo Venezia in Rome). The Medici collection was also renowned. It was started by Cosimo the Elder, and later was enlarged by his grandson Lorenzo by acquisition of some extraordinary specimens, such as the Farnese Cup. The collection was eventually given to Margherita of Austria, the mother of Alexander Farnese. The collection of Fulvio Orsini (1528-1600), is one of the most remarkable corpora to be incorporated into the Farnese collection. This renowned scholar was the librarian of Paul III Farnese. His collection was bequeathed to Charles III of Bourbon by the last Duke of Parma, and then transferred to Naples in 1735 to be displayed at the Royal Villa of Capodimonte. These Renaissance collections were put together to serve as treasures, as well as repositories of culture and prestige. When finances were low, the precious stones could be pawned and credit could be obtained from banks at favourable rates. Between the end of the 16th century and the end of the 17th century, the collection included just over 500 gems, some of which eventually ended up in northern European collections under mysterious circumstances. Little is known about the origins and acquisition dates of the other gems, both ancient and modern, that make up the collection today.

The Farnese Cup, detail

## The Farnese Cup

This example of Hellenistic glyptic art is unique, both in terms of its size and its magnificence. The Farnese Cup was made of a single piece of sardonyx, a hard stone also known as onyx. It was produced at the Ptolemaic Egyptian court and from there taken to Rome after Octavian's victory over Cleopatra. On the outside of the cup, there is a depiction in relief of a Gorgon head, a symbol of royal power Inside, eight characters are grouped to form an allegorical scene set in Egypt. This setting is revealed by the presence at the bottom of a sphinx in profile, upon which sits Isis (or, perhaps more likely, a Ptolemaic queen depicted in the guise of Isis) holding a sheaf of wheat in her hand. Triptolemos strides forward behind her. In Egyptian religion he can be identified with Horus, the son of Isis. The seed bag belongs to him, and with his hands he guides the handle and blade of a plough. Above him are two male figures representing the beneficent Etesian winds. To the left is depicted an old man, semi-draped and seated. He can be identified as a personification of the Nile, or, perhaps more likely, Hades-Dionysus-Osiris-Serapis. Finally, on the right, there are two girls, holding a cup and a cornucopia (horn of plenty). A traditional interpretation of the scene might restrict itself to viewing it as an allegorical celebration of the Nile's fertility. It may be appropriate, employing a different and more complex reading of the piece, to set alongside this interpretation another, namely a celebration of the ruling dynasty, depicted as a form of political propaganda. There is much debate over the identification of the three central figures as historical individuals, as members of the Lagid dynasty (Cleopatra I, Cleopatra III with her husband Ptolemy VIII (who died in 116 BC) and their son Ptolemy X Alexander, or Cleopatra VII). The most likely view suggests that this superb cup be dated to the 30s BC, viewing it as a celebration of the reign of Cleopatra VII as a period of peace and prosperity, an *aurea aetas* ('Golden Age'), destined to meet a tragic end shortly afterwards.

The high quality of the workmanship of the Farnese Cup means that since ancient times it has been a much vaunted treasure in royal courts, from that of the Pteolemies to Imperial Rome, and those of Byzantium, Frederick II, Persia and Aragon, and, in recent times, of the Medici and Farnese families.

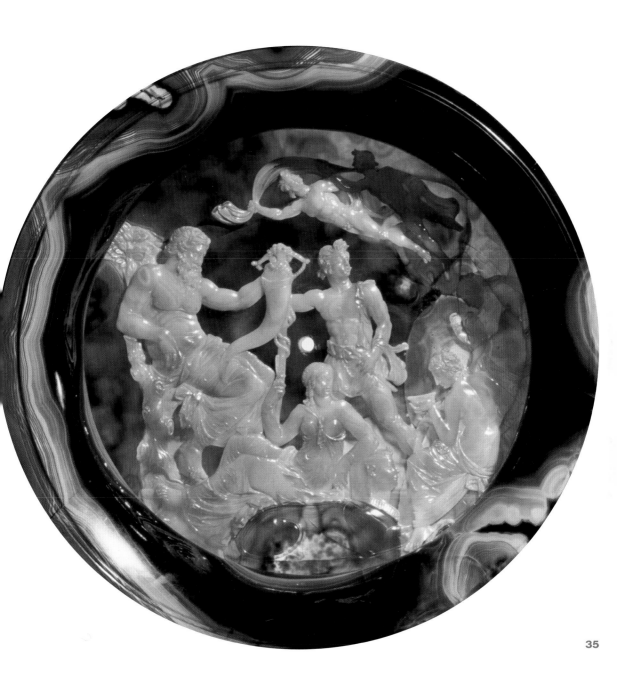

# ground floor

## The Greco-Roman sculpture of Campania

Located in the west wing on the ground floor, this section houses the statues and inscriptions of the Roman period that were discovered in the cities of Campania, and in particular in Pompeii, Herculaneum, Cuma and in the Phlegrean area. Of particular interest, because of their fame and importance are the honorific statues from Pompeii, the cult images of the Capitolium of Cuma, and the sculptures of the Palazzo Imperiale at Baiae and the Phlegrean villas. Today these works are still arranged according to the criteria established at the beginning of the 20th century by Ettore Pais, in line with the canons of the great German archaeological school of the 19th century. In particular, the rooms hold Roman imperial copies of classical Greek originals. These include the Athenian group of the Tyrannicides, the Sosandra Aphrodite and the Apollo of the *omphalos* by Kalamis, the Doryphorus by Polycleitus, the Athena, Hera and Nemesis by Agoracritus. Only a few original pieces survive, such as two magnificent statues of Nereids on mythological fish (*opera nobilia* from a villa at Formia) and an Attic relief with sacred scenes linked to the Eleusian mysteries from a villa in the territory of Sinuessa (modern Mondragone).

36

Diomedes of Cuma, detail

**Aphrodite of Capua**
The goddess is depicted semi-nude, with elaborate drapery that covers only her lower body, and with her foot planted on Ares' helmet. She is looking at her reflection in Ares' shield, which the statue must originally have held, raised up in both hands. Originally intended to decorate the portico of the *summa cavea* of the Capua amphitheatre, the statue is a Hadrianic reworking of a famous Greek model in bronze of the late classical period (end of the 4th century BC). The style is similar to the Venus-Victoria of Brescia of the Augustan period, and was originally intended to depict Venus the Victor, founder of the imperial family, writing the epic exploits of the Julian family on the shield of Mars; it was later transformed into the Victoria Caesaris ('Victory of Caesar') by the addition of wings.

### *Doryphorus* (spear-bearer)

This statue was found in 1797 in the Samnite Palaestra at Pompeii. It is one of the best surviving copies of a bronze original of the Classical period, the latter attributed to Polycleitus (440 BC). The bronze statue was known in antiquity as *Kanon,* symbolising the principles of harmony and proportion that the sculptor himself had described in a written work of the same name. The position of the figure is based on the chiastic pattern (from the form of the letter X, the Greek *chi*) described by the master. The right leg is held straight with the opposite left arm bent, the right arm extended. The figure of the young spearman, once thought to be Achilles, perfectly embodied the athletic and military ideals of the ruling classes of Athens during that period. The statue was found in 1797 near the Samnite Palaestra of Pompeii among the sculptural ornamentation that was part of the Augustan reconstruction of the complex. This period saw the revival of works of the Classical period, especially those by Polycleitus. Thus the achievement of perfection in the representation of the human form was assured.

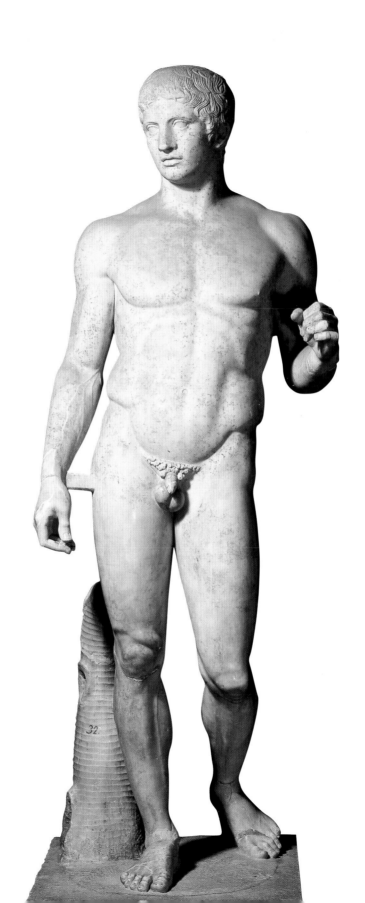

**Sosandra Aphrodite**
This statue of Aphrodite was discovered during excavations of the Baths of Baia. The goddess wears the *chiton* and mantle that cover her from her head to her lower legs and conceal her body entirely, except for the oval of her face. The statue was found at Baia in the excavations of the 1950s in the bath-theatre-nympheum complex and was probably never completed, since its surface is unfinished. It is an early imperial copy of a bronze original of Severe Style, datable to c. 465 BC. Its popularity in antiquity is highlighted by the existence of over 20 replicas. The original was the work of *Kalamis*, the Greek master of Boetian origin, and was displayed on the Acropolis of Athens, at the entrance to the Propyleum (Lucian, *Imagines* 4.6).

**Diomedes of Cuma**

This statue was found at Cuma during excavations in 1925, in the crypt beneath the Acropolis. It may originally have been dedicated in the Temple of Apollo. It depicts Diomedes, nude except for a cloak over his right shoulder; in his hands he probably held a sword and a model of the Palladium, the statue of Athena that was a symbol of Troy's inviolability, stolen by Ulysses. Many cities in Italy claimed to have noble Trojan origins based on possession of the Palladium that Diomedes brought with him to the Italian peninsula. The statue is an imperial copy of a Greek original attributed to the sculptor *Kresilas* (430 BC). It has an inscription in Greek on its base that gives the name of the man who may have dedicated it, Gaius Claudius Piso.

**Jupiter from Cuma**

This larger than life-sized statue depicts Jupiter seated on his throne, nude, with a cloak hanging from his shoulders to cover his legs. It was found near the so-called Masseria del Gigante at Cuma during excavations in 1758. Originally it was located at the back of the main cella of the *Capitolium* of the city, where Jupiter was venerated alongside Juno and Minerva (the Capitoline Triad). These were acrolithic statues: only the uncovered parts of the body (the face, hands and feet) were of marble. The rest was made up of a wooden framework to which were fixed drapes of real fabric or stucco, or sometimes even metal parts. The statue was also known by the name 'Giant of the Palazzo', since for a long time it was located in the so-called 'Stairway of the Giant' next to the Royal Palace of Naples. Set on a column within a stucco setting, it supported the Spanish royal coat of arms.

# basement

## The Egyptian Collection

The Egyptian collection of the Naples Museum is the second most important in Italy. It was formed from several different collections. Only one piece belonged to the Farnese Collection, the Naophoros statue, called, appropriately, 'Farnese'. The majority of the collection is that of the wealthy 18th century collector, Cardinal Stefano Borghese. It was purchased in 1815 by Ferdinand IV of Bourbon (Rooms 18-20). More recent are the collections of the 19th century Venetian traveler, Giuseppe Picchianti, who explored the Nubian desert (Rooms 21-22), and that of the German Schnars (Room 20, case 15), who visited many sites in Upper and Lower Egypt. Besides these collections a specific section is dedicated to Egyptian finds discovered in the cities of Campania (Room 21), providing evidence of the close relationship between Rome and Egypt, which began in the Ptolemaic period and endured for the whole of the 2nd century B.C. Pompeii, Herculaneum, Naples, Sorrento and Beneventum have yielded numerous Egyptian and Egytianizing sculptures and objects, used both in the ritual of the Isiac sanctuaries, and also as mere decorative objects, reflecting the fashion that spread all over the Roman world after the conquest of Egypt. Of particular note within this rich collection are mummy fragments and several Canopic vases, containers used to hold the internal organs of the deceased. The organs were removed from the body before mummification and placed into these vases bearing the name of the deceased that were then placed alongside the sarcophagus. The vases are shaped as the heads of the sons of Horus: the human head (Amset) contained the stomach and the intestine, the baboon head (Hapy) the small intestine, the jackel head (Duamutef) the lungs, and the falcon (Qebensenuf) the liver and gallbladder. The *shabti* collection is also remarkable. It comprises stone, wood and faience mummy-shaped statuettes representing entities required to work in the afterworld in the place of the deceased. Large numbers of them were gathered together (up to 365, one for each day of the year, with an overseer) and placed in a box in the tomb.

46

Funerary Stele of the Scribe Hui,
detail

# basement

## The Epigraphic Collection

The epigraphic section hosts one of the most important collections of inscriptions from the Greco-Roman world. Indeed, it brings together several important collections: that of the Farnese family (which itself had been merged with the collection created by Fulvio Orsini, the family's librarian); the Borgia collection, formed in Latium and Umbria; that of Francesco Daniele, the learned 18th century Campanian; and that of Monsignor Carlo Maria Rossini, of material from the area of the Phlegraean Fields. To these collections were added the finds from countless excavations and discoveries made in Campania and other parts of the Mezzogiorno of Italy from the 18th century until today. This means that rare epigraphic evidence has been gathered together relating to aspects of public and private life that are usually hard to document. This evidence includes the wax tablets from the archive of the Pompeian banker L. Caecilius Jucundus, electoral posters and announcements of gladiatorial games, and graffiti on plaster.

The first part of the collection (Room 150) is dedicated to evidence in Greek, with texts from different colonies in south Italy. The following room (Room 151) gathers together inscriptions from Naples, where Greek remained the official language until the end of the Roman Empire. The collection of inscriptions in pre-Roman languages of central and southern Italy (Etruscan, Oscan, Vestian, Volscian, Sabellic) is exceptional: (Rooms 151 and 152): of particular note is the Sabellic inscription from Bellante dating to the mid 6th century BC, and the 4th century Volscian inscription from Velletri. Room 153 holds political and institutional inscriptions (the *Tabula Bantina*, the *Lex agraria* of 111 BC and the *Lex Acilia repetundarum*, written on the same bronze sheet, and the *lex* Cornelia *de XX Quaestoribus* of 81 BC as set down by the Senate). There are also religious inscriptions here, such as the Orphic tablets of *Thurii* and votive cippi from the sanctuary of Persephone at Locri. Finally (Rooms 154 and 155) there is a selection of the huge numbers of inscriptions that have been found during the excavations of the Vesuvian cities and in the settlements of the Phlegrean area.

50

One of the Heraclea Tablets, detail

ΕΦΟΡΟΣΔΑΙΜΟΣΙΑΠΟΛΙΣ
ΚΑΙΤΟΙΟΡΙΣΤΑΙ ΕΣΤΡΙΠΟΥΣ ΦΙΛΩ
ΝΥΜΟΣΙΩΠΥΡΙΣΚΩ ΠΕΚΑΡΥΚΕΙΟΝ
ΑΠΟΛΛΩΝΙΟΣ ΗΡΑΚΛΗΤΩΙΑΙ ΠΕΛ
ΤΑ ΔΑΙΜΟΣΙΥΡΡΩΑΘΑΝΑΙΠΟΛΙΑΔΙ

ΑΝΕΓΡΑΨΑΝΤΟΙΟΡΙΣΤΑΙΤΟΙΑΙΡΕΘΕΝΤΕΣΕΠΙΤΩΣΧΩΡΩΣΤΩΣ
ΑΛΕΩΝΙΟΣ ΗΡΑΚΛΗΤΩΔΑΙΜΟΣΙΠΥΡΡΩ ΟΔΟΙ ΚΑΙΣΥΝΕΝΕ
ΜΟΝΤΩΝ ΕΝΚΑΓΑΚΛΗΤΔΙΑΛΙΑΙΣΥΝΕΜΕΤΡΗΣΑΜΕΣΔΕΑΡΞΑΛΕΙ
ΚΟΝΤΑΤΙΕΔΟΝΤΑΝΕΠΙΘΟΛΑΣΣΑΝΑΠΟΣΑΝΚΑΙΕΓΕΝΟΝΤΟΣΑΠΟ
ΑΝ ΙΕΠΙΤΑΤΥΓΑΙΑΤΤΟΔΕΤΑΣΚΟΥΒΗΤΙΝΤΑΝΑΙΑΤΩΝΠΥΑΝΕΚΤΟΛΟΣΡΕΩ
ΕΝΝΕΑΣΤΥΗΜΙΓΥΑ ΔΙΑΛΑΝΤΕΣΜΕΤΑΝΤΙΑΚΟΝΤΑΤΑΤΕΔΟΝΤΑΝ
ΤΥΙΑΜΕΣΤΟΡΙΤΟΝΕΙΚΑΤΙΔΕΙΟΝ ΚΑΤΕΜΕΤΤΗΣΑΜΕΣΤΟΝΕΙΚΑ
ΤΟΝΤΡΙΗΜΙΓΥΟΝΤΑΣΑΡΓΙΑΟΥΚΕΣΕΣΤΟΟΝΚΑΠΩΣΤΟΑΜΠΕΛΩΝ
ΠΥΡΙΣΚΟΜΕΣΤΕΓΕΝΗΜΕΛΥΑΛΛΩΣ ΡΕΙΟΗΜΙΓΥΟΝΜΟΝΟΙΚΑ
ΤΑΡΕΙΤΙΕ ΤΟ ΕΚΤΩΝ ΟΥΟΝ ΤΡΙΜΙΓΥΟΝΤΑΙ ΕΛΟΙΤΑΝΡΑΝΕΙΔΙΑΝ
ΙΕΣΕΤΤΕΠΟΙΗΝΤΟ ΤΑΥΤΑΝ ΑΠΕΚΑΤΕΣΤΑΣΑΜΕΣΤΑΙΑ
ΤΤΑΑΡΧΑΙΑ ΑΠΟΛΑΒΤΩΣΙΚΑΤΙΔΕΙΟΤΑΝΕΣΕΟΤΙΛΑΠΟΝΥ
ΙΤΟΤΙΡΕΝΟΜΕΝΑΝΤΑΝΕΜΙΜΕΣ Λ ΤΑΣΤΕΕΚΑΤΟΝΤΕΔΩ
ΑΙΤΑΣΡΗΓΑΚΛΕΙΑΣΡΟΔΑ ΚΑΙΤΑΥΤΑΙΠΑΣΑΝΕΠΙΔΙΑΝΕΤΙΕΤΟΙΗΝΩ
ΙΝΕΣ ΚΑΙΤΟΙΜΕ ΜΕΤΡΕΑΝΤΕΣΑΤΙΕ ΡΕΝΤΟΙΣΑΛΣΟΙΚ ΝΕΣΑΜΕΘ ΝΑΚΑ
ΙΑΚΟΣΤΑΙΑΣΚΑΙΑΠΟΚΑΙΑΣΤΑΞΑΝΤΕΣΤΑΙΘΕΛΙΚΑΝΤΑ
ΑΝΤΑΝΓΩΝΚΑΤΕΛΑΣΣΑΜΕΘΑΚΑΙΟ ΕΣ ΕΠΑΞΑΜΕΣ ΕΚΑΣΤΟΣ ΤΑΣ
ΙΛΟΣ ΚΑΙΕΠΟΙΗΣΑΜΕΣΤΙΑΤΟΤΡΙΗΥΜΙΓΥΟΝ ΟΔΕΚΑΤΟΝΤΡΑΤΟΝΤΙ
ΟΝΤΤΟΘΕΝΤΕΣΤΙΤΤΑΤΕΙ ΗΜΙΓΥΟΝ ΛΑΣΚΑΤΕΠΟΙ ΕΣΤΑΣΙΟΙ
ΙΜΕΝ ΕΚΠΛΕΟΝΕΥΡΩΣΤΥΓΥΟΝΙΝ Κ ΞΑΠΟΤΑΣΗΚΑ ΤΑ ΑΥΧΙΠΟΤ
ΑΡΗΓΑΚΛΕΑΝΠΟΘΕ ΝΑΝΤ ΘΜΙΣ ΚΑΙΕΣΕΝΟΙ ΣΧΟΝΟΙ ΣΡ Π ΤΟΝΤΗ
ΤΟΝΟΚΤ ΦΙΛΑΣΜΕ ΕΚΑΤΟΝ ΤΡΙΗΚΟ ΤΑΤΗΣ Ο ΡΕΜΑΤΑΕΙΚΑΤ
ΙΕΤΕΤΥΣΑΜΠΕΛΩΝΑΣΤΕΤΟΥΕΣΣ ΟΙΝΟΙΟΡΕ ΜΑΤΑΔΕΚΑ ΕΠΤΑΔΕΣ
ΤΗΣΡΑΥΤΑΓΑΓΑΕΜΙΣΟΛΔΙΗΤΑΝΤΡΙΑΤΑΙΤΕΙ Τ Σ ΕΠΙΗ ΚΑΙ ΙΑΚΟΝΤΑΝ
ΕΞΗΚΟΝΤΑΕΝΝΕΑΜΕΔΙΜΝΩΝΧΟΟΣΔΥΑΝΧΟΙΝΙΚ Ι Σ ΟΔΕΤΟΥΤΩ
ΤΡΙΓΩΕΜΕΤΡΗΣΑΜΕΣΤΟΤΤΟΕΠΙΚΑΤΙΔΕΙΟ ΔΕΥΤΕΡΑΣΤΡΙΓΥΟΙ
ΞΑΝΤΩΣΡΟΣΜΑΚΟΣΑΠΟΤΑΣΡΕΚΑΤΟΝΤΕΔΑΤΟΤΙΡ ΝΗΗΡΑΚΛΕΙ
ΑΩΝ ΚΑΙΕΓΕΝΟΝΤΟΣΧΟΙΝΟΙ ΕΚΑΤΟΝ ΤΡΙΑΚΟΝΤΑ ΕΝΝΕΑ ΗΜΙ ΣΜΕΙ
ΤΟΝΟΙΚΑΤΙΤΡΙΣΣΧΟΙΝ Ι ΛΑΝΡΕΧΟΝ ΔΕ ΔΕΚΑΕΙΣ ΣΧΟΙΝΟΙΤΟΥΤΟΤΟΣ
ΤΟΙΕΜΙΣ ΟΘΗ ΣΕΦΑΛΧΟΙ ΡΕΝΕΝΗΚΟΝΤΑΤΩΝΓΕΝΕΔΙΜΝΩΝ
ΑΙΑΒΑΝΤΩΣΔΕ ΤΙ ΕΙΚΑΤΙΔΕΙΟΝ ΕΠΟΙΗΣΑΜΕΣΤΡΙΑΤΑΝΜΕΡΙΔΑ ΤΑΤ
ΝΤΕΣΔΟΝ ΕΝΑΙΓΡΑΜΠΕΛΑ ΡΗΙ Κ ΚΑΙΕΤ Σ ΟΜΕΣΚΟΙΝ ΝΤΟΟΔΑΡΝΕΙΣ
ΑΤΑΣ ΥΛΑΡΕΣΠΟΤΑΜΟΝ Ι ΤΑΤΕΛΟΝΕ ΑΙΣΡΕΤΙΟΝ ΕΣ ΑΥΤΟΤΕΣΕΙΚΑΤ
ΤΟΤΑΚΙ ΙΝΕΠΙΤΑΝΔΙΑΣΤΟΛΑΝΤΑΝΤΙΑΡ ΓΑΝΤΑΝΑΠΥΤΑΣΠΟΦΟΔΑ Σ ΤΑΣ
ΙΕΡΑΓΟΡΑΣΕΣΤΑΝΡΕΚΑΤΟΝΠΕΔΟΝΚΑΙΕΓΕΝΟΝΤΟΠΕΝΤΗΡΟΝΤΑ ΕΝΝΕ
ΝΤ ΗΜΙΣΧΟΙΝΟΝ ΛΑΣΜΕΝΤΕΝΤΗΚΟΝΤΑΜΙΑ ΓΡΑΜΜΑΤΑΗΕΠΤΑΑΜΠΕΛ
ΗΟΣΤΤ ΣΧΟΙΝ Ι ΤΑΙΟΝΕΣΤΑΙΤΑΙΕΜ ΟΘΗΤΕΤΡΑΚΑΤΙΟΝΤΕΣΑ
ΤΑΣ ΙΕΔΙΜΕΝ Ι ΤΟΑΙΧΩΝ ΣΣΑΡΩΝ ΔΕΥΤΕΡΑΜΕΡΙΞΕΝΗΑΙΡΑΟΣ
ΣΤ ΜΑΚΟΣΑΠΟΤΟΣΙΚ ΤΙ ΑΕΙΣ ΕΠΙΤΑΝ ΤΡΑ ΟΙΤΑΝΠΑΡΠΟΤΑΜΟΝ ΕΥΡΟΣ ΑΤΟ
ΑΝ ΚΑΙΤΑΣΠΟΦΟΛΩΤΑΣ ΙΟΙ ΤΑΙ ΕΧΟΝΤΑΣ ΡΕ Μ ΝΑΤ ΛΑΣΑΣΕΠΙΤΟΣΟ
ΙΕ ΓΕΝΟΝ ΤΟΒΕΞΗΚΟΝΤ ΡΕΣΧΟΙΝΟΙΟΡΕ ΜΑΤΑ ΔΕΚΑΛΟΤΑΥΤΑΙ ΤΑ ΙΜΕΡ
ΙΣΤΕΛΑΣΣΑΜΕΘΑΜΠΕΛ ΝΤΡΙ ΤΑΝΔΙ Σ ΟΛΑΝΤΑΝΤΙΑΡ ΤΑΝ ΕΚΑΤΟΝ ΤΕ
ΕΟΚΤΩΣΧΟΙΝ ΩΣ ΟΡΕ ΤΑ ΕΙΚΑΤΙΕΞΡΟΔ Σ ΟΥΚΑΙΕΓΕΝΕΤΟΙΑΠΑΣΑΝΕΡ

### The Heraclea Tablets

The Heraclea Tablets consist of two bronze sheets, inscribed on both sides with text in Greek and Latin from different periods. They were discovered in 1732 in a river bed in the countryside between Heraclea and Metaponto in the Basilicata region, in a place that recently has been identified as the likely meeting place of the federal assembly of the Italiot League, and which must, therefore, have been the site of the public archive of Heraclea. The two Greek inscriptions date to between the end of the 4th century and beginning of the 3rd century BC and set out the rules of the city of Heraclea concerning the reappropriation, distribution and redistribution for rent of sacred land belonging to the sanctuaries of Athena Polias and Dionysus. This had been illegally occupied by private citizens (members of important local families) and later brought back into the control of the city. The document is of extraordinary importance in reconstructing the agrarian economy of the Greek colonies of Ionic Lucania, which was dominated by cultivation of cereals (wheat, spelt and, in particular, barley), vines and olives.

### Orphic inscriptions from Thurii

These two groups of inscribed gold *laminae* from 4th century BC burials found in the territory of *Thurii* belong to a wider class of Greek inscriptions with a funerary function. They are very small in size and have been found in the tombs of Magna Grecia, in Crete, in Thessaly and at Rome. The inscriptions are instructions: their purpose was to lead the souls of the deceased, initiates of a mystery doctrine that went back to Orpheus, to their final promised destiny of eternal blessing at the end of their cycle of reincarnation. The gold sheets, folded in four or rolled up, may have been kept in cylindrical containers attached like pendants to necklaces placed on the deceased, or placed directly in funerary urns (*hydriae*) containing the ashes of the deceased. Sometimes they were placed open in the right hand of the deceased, or even deposited inside the mouth of the corpse. The examples from *Thurii* belong to a lower class mystery sect which had some knowledge of the Orphic-Pythagoric orthodoxy.

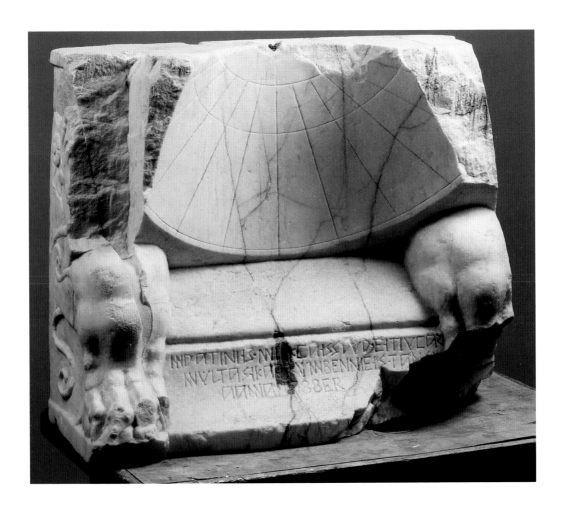

## Sundial from the Stabian Baths

The inscription on the sundial tells us, in Oscan, that it was set up by the quaestor Maras Atinis, with money raised from fines paid by citizens. The earliest sundial was introduced to Rome from Catania by Marcus Valerius Messalla in 263 BC and set up in the Comitium of the Republican Forum. Before that date the Comitium itself – of rectangular shape and oriented to the cardinal points – had functioned as a giant sundial, permitting the heralds to identify the most important moments of the day: dawn, noon and sunset.

# mezzanine floor

## The Mosaic Collection

The majority of the mosaic floors of black and white tesserae found at Pompeii and Herculaneum were used in the mid-18th century to pave the rooms of the new royal structures built by the Bourbons (the Herculanense Museum in the Villa of Portici, the Palace of Capodimonte, and the Palazzo degli Studi). Mosaic panels were rarer, and for them a different fate was accorded. Together with the gems and other precious objects, they were placed in a kind of 'room of marvels'. In 1826 the director of the Museum decided to gather the mosaics and ancient paintings into a small collection in a room on the ground floor. The discovery of the extraordinary mosaics from the House of the Faun in Pompeii (1830-1832) enriched the collection, and between 1910 and 1924 the mosaics were separated from the frescoes and displayed according to the material and technique of their design. A reorganization in 2001 was based on the same principles and located in five rooms (54-59)

The collection is among the finest in existence, above all on account of the exceptional finds from the Vesuvian cities. It is still almost entirely displayed according to the museological principles of the 19th century, which tended to separate material according to different classes of artistic production and ignore provenance. The collection will eventually be reorganized to reunite groups from particular contexts.

The Alexander mosaic, detail

**Emblema depicting the passing of life (a so-called memento mori)**
This is a Second Style mosaic that formed the central motif (*emblema*) of the *triclinium* of a house in Pompeii. It presents, in allegorical form, the philosophical theme, itself of Hellenistic origin, of life's passing and death as the leveller of human fortunes. At the centre of the composition is a level; the weight on the plumb-line is death (the skull). Beneath this are a butterfly (the soul) and a wheel (fate). On the left hand side are symbols of wealth and power (a sceptre and purple cloak); on the right, symbols of poverty (a beggar's pack and walking-stick).

## The mosaics of Dioskourides

These two fine mosaics panels bear the signature of Dioskourides. They were found in the so-called Villa of Cicero discovered in Pompeii in 1763, immediately outside the Herculaneum Gate, and subsequently re-buried. Influenced by Hellenistic art of the 3rd century BC, the first mosaic portrays street musicians, whereas the second depicts a consultation with a sorceress, a scene inspired by the plot of a comedy by Menander.

## Mosaic *emblema* depicting a group of itinerant musicians

This panel depicts a group of four individuals on a stage, on their way to the door of a house (visible to the right of the scene) accompanied by the music of a tambourine and a double flute. They are wearing the masks of three characters from New Comedy. The tambourine player is the *parasitos*, behind him is the *kolax* (flatterer), playing the cymbals, then the *diamitros etera*, playing the double flute, followed by a boy playing a horn. The use of *chiaroscuro* and of shadow suggest that the panel is an original of the Alexandrian School (3rd century BC), signed by *Dioskurides Samios*.

**The mosaics of the House of the Faun at Pompeii**

These mosaics are without doubt the most precious objects in the Naples Collection, both in terms of the quality and richness of their subjects, and due to the fame that followed their discovery and excavation. The traditional name of the house derives from the famous bronze statuette of the Dancing Faun (although in the 19th century it was named after Goethe, or known as the house of the 'Grand Mosaic' of Alexander). The Faun is a clear and direct reference to the Hellenistic court of Alexandria in Egypt and to its rich iconographic repertoire, full of references to the Dionysian and theatrical sphere. From the moment of its discovery, the Faun was subject of admiration and renown, so much so that an English traveler in 1838 wrote: "it is not the most marvelous statue in the world because a Faun is not the most marvelous creature in the world... It is, however, the Venus de' Medici of the Sylvans, begging forgiveness for this change of species".

The luxurious mosaic panels (*emblemata*) provide reference to the colourful world of Dionysus and the Greek theatre adorned a number of rooms in the house: the threshold between the entrance vestibule of the house and its Tuscan atrium (an *emblema* with a rich festoon of flowers and fruit adorned by two tragic female masks with long curly wigs); a room next to the atrium (a double *emblema* depicting a cat capturing a partridge and Nilotic ducks with lotus flowers in their beaks); the banquet halls (an *emblema* depicting Dionysus as a child riding a tiger in the centre of a vegetal frame with theatrical masks, and an *emblema* depicting marine fauna centred on a lobster capturing a squid); and a bedroom (an erotic *emblema* depicting Satyr and Nymph).

The mosaic threshold of the exedra of the grand mosaic recalls an exotic Egyptian scene, with a representation of a Nilotic landscape filled with ducks, snakes, crocodiles and hippopotami. The scene introduces the main decorative theme of the hall, which centres on the celebration of Alexander and the foundation of Alexandria. It constitutes a monumental mosaic depicting the battle which assured Alexander's conquest of Asia, and his arrival in the rich Delta region.

The rich mosaic decoration of the House of the Faun is the work of skilled Alexandrian craftsmen, active in Italy between the end of the 2nd century BC and the beginning of the 1st century BC. This was the period in which this Pompeian 'palace' was renovated; the size and magnificence of its plan recall the splendour of eastern Hellenistic palaces. The Pompeian mosaics are dated with reference to the writings of Pliny the Elder who referred to the custom of inserting medallions into the centre of the mosaic floor. These medallions (*emblemata*) were made separately of tiny coloured tesserae, a practice documented in Rome from the second half of the 2nd century BC (*Natural History*, 36.61).

58

## The Alexander mosaic

This large scale (5.82 x 3.13 m) mosaic is one of the most famous works of art to have come down to us from antiquity. It was found on 24 October 1831 in the House of the Faun at Pompeii, where it decorated a rectangular colonnaded exedra on one side of the central peristyle of the house. The scene depicted is one of the battles between Alexander the Great, who charges bare-headed from left to right, and Darius III (in flight in his chariot, on the right). This famous mosaic is an precise copy of one of the great paintings of the early Hellenistic period (the second half of the 4th century BC). There is great debate over the identification of the original painting, whether it was a panel painting by Philoxenos of Eretria, painted for king Cassander and in all likelihood displayed in the Macedonian royal palace at Pella; or whether it is a work by the Egyptian painter Helena, daughter of Timon, depicting the battle of Issus. The breadth of conception of this composition is unprecedented, with the masses of men and horses caught up in frenzied motion, highlighted by the juxtaposition of the long lances against the light sky. The painting must have been very famous in antiquity, and was copied on Etruscan urns and in relief on ceramic cups. The technique used for the Pompeian mosaic is the highly sophisticated *opus vermiculatum*. It is made up of about a million tesserae, with 15 to 30 tesserae per square centimeter.

# mezzanine floor

## The Secret Cabinet

From the Renaissance, collections of 'obscene' objects were considered a fundamental part of any collection of antiquities. At times kept hidden, or concealed in private rooms or in 'gardens of Love' such as the one in the Villa Farnese, these statues, gems, lamps and paintings were a source of artistic inspiration, provoked forgeries and erudite essays, and aroused simply hot-blooded curiosity throughout the period in which aristocratic collections were fashionable. The embarrassment of the Bourbon excavators of Pompeii and Herculaneum at the discovery of explicit erotica is echoed in contemporary documents (comparing the immorality of Pompeii to the legendary Sodom) and in the decision made to reserve a "closed" room for the display of these artefacts in the Herculanean Museum of Portici. This room was accessible only to the few who managed to obtain a special permit from Court functionaries. The more liberal approach of those behind the new museum at Palazzo degli Studi, who decided to display the "secret" collection to the public, was soon curtailed by an upsurge of moralism that followed a visit to the Museum by the daughter of Francis I. It was for this reason that a specific "Private Room of Obscene Objects" was created and opened only to those "persons of a mature age and a well-known morality". At the time, the collection contained 102 objects which were "infamous monuments of heathen licentiousness." During the years of the revolution, those who wanted permission to the room to be granted more widely were opposed by others who wanted to prevent the display even of the nude or semi-nude Venuses in the Naples Museum. As often happens, the reactionary spirit triumphed and the artefacts were hidden away on the first floor and forgotten by most. Since that time, the Secret Room has been opened or closed according to political circumstances: it was reopened in the years that followed Garibaldi's arrival in Naples, but was semi-closed again by the Savoy government and by the Fascist regime and remained closed until 1967.

Tripod with satyrs, detail.
From the House of Julia Felix in Pompeii

**Marble group of Pan and goat**

This sculptural group was found in the course of the 1752 excavation of the Villa of the Papyri at Herculaneum, where it decorated the so-called Grand Peristyle. It is an early imperial copy of a Hellenistic original. It depicts Pan, the Arcadian god of the woodlands (half-goat in form – only the upper half of his body is human) in the act of coupling with a she-goat. The subject matter is perfectly suited to the decoration of a villa garden, where Romans delighted in the depiction of nature filled with the pastoral-idyllic connotations so familiar from Hellenistic literature and art. Despite its lightness of tone, the coarseness of the subject matter in the eyes of Bourbon society meant that this was, perhaps, one of the most heavily censored objects in the collection. Only the king was allowed to see it before it was shut away in a cupboard, hidden even from the eyes of Winckelmann. The opinion of Valadier, who described it as a work "most lascivious, but beautiful" is one shared by many.

### *Tintinnabulum* in the shape of an ithyphallic gladiator

Bronze *tintinnabulum* of the early imperial period, found at Herculaneum during the excavations of 1740. It has four bells attached to chains, and a gladiator at the centre. The gladiator's headdress is made up of strips of some kind of material, and he wears a short tunic and sandals; he is fighting his own phallus, which has turned into a panther with mouth wide open, about to turn on him. Although sometimes used during sumptuous banquets to summon different courses, these objects were more commonly hung from the doors of private houses and, particularly, of shops. Their function was to signal the entrance of visitors and ward off the evil eye.

# mezzanine floor

## The Coin and Medal Collection

The Museum has a magnificent collection of over 200,000 coins and medals. Some come from the original Farnese Collection, patiently put together by the humanist Fulvio Orsini as part of his study of antique iconography and imperial portraiture (the so-called Imperial Series). Others come from the Bourbon excavations in the Vesuvian cities, in Magna Grecia and in Sicily. To these rich discoveries, made in those early years of archaeology, have been added private coin collections, particularly the Santangelo Collection (with more than 42,000 pieces) acquired by the Museum of Naples in 1864. The first room (Room 51) is dedicated to the history of numismatics and coin collecting and has a small but important selection from the Museum's private collections. The second room (Room 52) contains coins from some of the most important Greek colonies in southern Italy and in Sicily (Sybaris, Tarentum, Rhegium, Messina), which document the different monetary systems in use. The Achaean system was based on a tridrachm of Corinthian origin weighing 8 grammes: the first coins minted are characterized by a special technique called *incusa,* that is they bear the same image in relief on the obverse that is stamped on the reverse; this technique later spread throughout Magna Grecia. The Chalcidian system was based on a drachma of about 5.70 grammes, and was adopted by the colonies of the straits of Messina (Naxos, Zankle-Messana, Rhegium) and other cities founded by Euboean colonists (Cuma and *Himera*). Other systems included the "Phocaean" one adopted by Velia, Poseidonia and subsequently by all the cities of Campania, based on a didrachm of 7.50 grammes, and the "Attic" system adopted by Syracuse, with tetradrachms of 17.20 grammes. Another distinctive feature of the coinage of Magna Graecia was the more frequent use of gold than in Greece; it was used in particular to pay mercenaries from regions such as Epirus and Macedonia where that metal was in general use.

The third room (Room 53) illustrates the monetary system of Campania, from the first issues of Cumae to the well-known series coined by Neapolis. A special section is devoted to the coins of Sicily, ranging from the oldest pieces from Selinunte, Agrigentum and Gela which date back to the second half of the 6<sup>th</sup> century BC, to later ones coined in Syracuse by the tyrant Dionysios I, with a bronze core and an elegantly engraved gold or silver exterior. The same tyrant was the instigator of a wide-ranging reform employing bronze coin for internal trade and gold or silver coin for trade with the outside world. The latter, of very high artistic quality, were entrusted to particularly skilled engravers such as *Kimon*, *Euaneitos* and *Euklidas*. The collection of Italic coins conserved in the Museum of Naples is just as noteworthy, from the primitive *aes rude* (unrefined metal used for exchange) to the system of Republican coins (the *as* and its denominations) and Augustan coins, including brass *sestertii* and *dupondii*, and the copper *as* and *quadrantes*.

In addition to the coins, other visual evidence is displayed here, painted and sculpted, which help to reconstruct the society and economy of the Vesuvian cities. This includes a marble relief depicting scenes from a coppersmith's shop, and paintings depicting everyday scenes such as the sale of bread, cooked food or work tools. Room 55 contains mediaeval evidence found in Campania and Sicily, and concludes with the monetary history of the Kingdom of the Two Sicilies from the Norman period up to the Bourbon dynasty.

**Incuse stater inscribed Ami, from Cittanuova**

On the obverse, in exergue, the inscription Ami; a bull, its body facing left, looking over its shoulder. Above it is a locust, below it a braided border. On the reverse, the same type, incuse. The rim of the coin has a border with a fish-spine motif. The coin (g 7.84), struck in silver, dates to 540-510 BC. The bull looking backwards is a type employed on the coinage of Sybaris and is reproduced in identical form on the coins of that Achaean city and its subcolonies.

**Decadrachm of Syracuse**

On the obverse a *quadriga* (four horse chariot) with a Victory crowning the charioteer; under the exergue border a trophy of arms; on the reverse, the head of Kore facing left, wreathed with ears of grain; around her are dolphins, below the signature of the engraver, Euainetos. Dated to 390 BC.

**Gold medallion of Augustus, from Pompeii**
Struck at the mint of Lyons (Lugdunum) in 9-8 BC, this medallion, found at Pompeii in 1759, has on its obverse the head of Augustus facing left, wearing a laurel wreath; on the reverse is the legend *Imp(erator) XV* and an image of a statue of Artemis that must have been well-known in Sicily (*Sicil* is written in the exergue), perhaps the famous statue of Diana of Segesta, depicted with her bow and in the act of drawing an arrow from her quiver.

# first floor

## The Villa of the Papyri

The Villa of the Papyri, with its extraordinary collections of almost 100 sculptures (65 works in bronze and 28 in marble) and more than 1,000 rolls of papyrus that were found during the 18th century excavations (1750-1754), is unique in the history of archaeology. There has always been a lively debate about the identification of the owner of the villa: the names of Lucius Calpurnius Piso Caesoninus, father-in-law of Julius Caesar and consul in 58 BC, his son (Lucius Calpurnius Piso Pontifex) who was consul in 15 BC, Appius Claudius Pulcher, brother-in-law of Lucullus and consul in 54 BC, and finally Marcus Octavius have been suggested. Recent studies favour Lucius Calpurnius Piso Caesoninus. Certainly the villa must have belonged to a rich and cultured member of the Roman *nobilitas* of the late Republican and early Augustan period. This can be determined from the exceptional collection of works of art and the extensive library of Greek and Latin papyri (1758 rolls). After almost two and a half centuries of study, the recent renewal of excavations has clarified some features of the plan of the villa (until these excavations only the parts of the villa tunneled by the Bourbons in the mid-18th century were known) and shed light on the decorative programme of the villa's sculpture. Portraits of famous men (kings, generals, philosophers and orators, and subjects deriving from Dionysiac (statues of satyrs and Pan) and gymnasium themes (statues of runners, statues of Hermes and Hercules) adorned the large peristyle, at the centre of which lay a swimming pool. The five bronze statues of the so-called Dancers were found near the *ambulacrum*, possibly recalling on a smaller scale the 50 daughters of Danaus that decorated the porticoes of the Temple of Apollo on the Palatine at Rome. The Dionysiac theme appears to dominate in the atrium (with numerous statues of Silenus, satyrs and cupids used as fountain-heads) along with references to the Hellenistic royal world (busts of kings such as Ptolemy II and Nicomedes I of Bithynia). It is more difficult to identify the sculptures found in the so-called *tablinum*. Many papyrus rolls were also found here, and it may have been a reading room for the texts that were stored in a nearby room. Consistent with this interpretation was the discovery of a series of eight bronze busts of Greek writers and philosophers (Epicurus, and perhaps Demosthenes) and of private individuals, possibly added later (the so-called Lepidus, the so-called Scipio, a possible portrait of Lucius Calpurnius Piso Pontifex) and a statue of *Athena Promachos*. In the square peristyle there were copies of Amazons attributed to Pheidias and of Polyceitus' *Doryphoros*. Opposite them was a pair of philosopher portraits. A bronze portrait of a Hellenistic king with stylised curls and the bronze head of the so-called Dionysus-Plato (most recently thought to be the god Priapus) were also located here.

68

Athena Promachos

## The daughters of Danaus

These five female bronze statues were identified as 'Dancers' by Winckelmann, and later as *hydrophorai* (water-carriers), but have been recognized recently as the daughters of Danaus, condemned to pour water perpetually as a punishment for having murdered their bridegrooms (and cousins) at their father's instigation, because he wanted to revenge himself on his brother Aegyptus. The most famous representation of this theme decorated the portico of the Roman Temple of Apollo Palatinus. There 50 statues of the girls and the same number of statues of their husbands on horseback symbolized Augustus' victory over Egypt after the battle of Actium. . The "Dancers" of Herculaneum probably served a similar evocative function. They were classical copies of the Augustan period of "Severe Style" sculptures. A very recent hypothesis suggests that they were located in the rectangular peristyle at the time of the eruption because restructuring work was taking place in the villa; their original location would have been along the edges of the *euripus* of the square peristyle.

## Epicurus

This small bronze bust of Epicurus is fundamental for the study of the image of this philosopher, because it can be identified securely from the inscription in Greek letters written on its base. It is one of a number of Roman copies of an original which historians believe was made immediately after the death of Epicurus (270 B.C.). Its presence in the Villa is not surprising: the philosophical ideals of the owner were all based on Epicurean doctrine which taught that life should be full of joy and pleasure and free from pain and worries; this philosophy was so far removed from the principles of the *polis* that those who followed it were called "those of the garden" (Sextus Empiricus, *Against Mathematicians*, 1.64).

## Pseudo-Seneca

Long thought by archaeologists to be a portrait of Seneca, (an idea first proposed by Fulvio Orsini in the 16th century), the bronze bust from the Villa of the Papyri must certainly portray one of the famous Greek poets (once, at least, it was considered to be the playwright Menander). The portrait is veristic, with "poor" and "age-worn" features. This is a face that expresses weariness for the sufferings of day-to-day living and hard work, but that is illuminated by an internal vigor and noble intellect. It is very similar to Hellenistic depictions of farmers and fishermen. Over the years different identifications have been proposed (Lucius Calpurnius Piso Caesoninus, Aristophanes, Epicharmus of Kos, Philemon of Syracuse, Hesiod and Ennius), none of which are considered entirely convincing today. The bust is an Augustan copy of a statue, made around 200 BC, which enjoyed great popularity. There are over 50 copies of it.

73

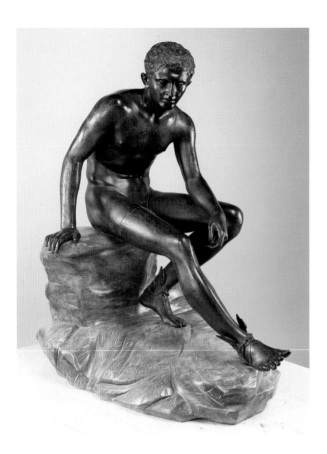

## Hermes at Rest

This bronze sculpture of Hermes at Rest (Hermes depicted as a seated youth), is part of the decoration of the grand peristyle, characterized by sophisticated references to Dionysiac religion and the ideals of the Greek gymnasium. It is a Roman copy of a Hellenistic original inspired by a Lysippan prototype. For many years it was thought that this was a replica of a work by Lysippus dating to the second half of the 4th century BC. A more convincing alternative is that the work was an eclectic creation, based on a famous Lysippan type, identified as the *Hermes* in Vienna. The image of this god was set across from that of *Athena* on the other side of the peristyle. It represents the Roman ideal of *otium*, the anthesis of the idea of *negotium* expressed in the statue of the goddess. Thus the two divinities form the key to understanding the peristyle, which is thought to be the gymnasium of the villa. The facial features, which were probably restored in antiquity, recall characteristics of portraits of the late Republic and the early Empire, suggesting that it was produced locally. Fortunately, it was returned to the Museum collections in 1947, after having been stolen from the Montecassino bomb shelter during the war.

## Runners

These statues depict nude life-size ephebes. They are about to start a running race, and have their left leg forward and their right one behind, with heel raised. In the past it was thought that the statues represented athletes engrossed in a wrestling match, or even discus-throwers. However, their interpretation as runners is now favoured. The setting of these two statues in the rectangular peristyle of the villa was intended to make the area seem like a gymnasium. The model from which the bronzes were copied must come from the Lysippan school, and can be dated to the end of the 4$^{th}$ and early 3$^{rd}$ century BC.

## Seleucus I

This bronze bust represents a man of middle years, his head inclined and circled with a band that is tied at the nape of the neck. It is generally accepted that this is a portrait of the founder-king of the Seleucid dynasty, Seleucus I, an identification based on comparison with portraits of the king on coins. It is more difficult to identify the original work of which this portrait is a copy; the original has been attributed to Lysippus, Aristodemus and, most recently, Tisicrates.

## Male bust (the so-called Ptolemy Apion)

This bust depicts a person with a distinctive hair style: the hair consists of individual wavy locks that hug the skull and are held in place by a ribbon at the nape of the neck. From the ribbon curls fall onto the forehead and around the neck. Since the time of its discovery this unusual bust has aroused count-less questions about the gender of the person depicted and his/her identification. In the 18th century the Herculanean Academy proposed that this was the king Ptolemy Apion; it has also been identified as Aulus Gabinius, consul in 58 BC; as *Thespis*, the flute-player who lived at the end of the 4th century BC at the court of Ptolemy I; and as one of the rulers of the kingdom of Arabia (whose image known from coins is very similar to this bust).

77

# first floor

## Greek Culture in the Bay of Naples

This section is dedicated to the history and archaeology of the Bay of Naples, from the first commercial exchanges with the Greek world to the foundation of the colonies of *Pithecusae*, Cumae and Naples itself, and finally to the revival of Hellenic styles and customs by Roman culture and society of the late Republic. The artefacts of pre-Hellenic Cumae, where locally produced vases were found in association with the imported Greek geometric vases, are followed by the establishment of the Greek emporium of *Pithecusae*, on the island of Ischia. Pithecusae was the oldest Greek settlement in the Western world, so remote as to be associated in the Hellenic imagination with 'a savage island, situated at the ends of the world and inhabited by monkeys'. The only evidence of the rich cultural exchanges that the Greek colonists, originally from the island of Euboea, had with the local populations is the wealth of grave goods found in the tombs excavated in the valley of San Montano. Today these are housed in the Naples Museum and the new Museum of Villa Arbusto at Lacco Ameno on Ischia. There is a wealth of evidence in the museum about the Greek colony of Cuma in the Museum. Cuma was founded some time after Pithecusae by the Euboeans. This was confirmed by the sporadic archaeological investigations of the 17th century that continued more systematically during the second half of the 19th century and the first decades of the 20th century, under the direction of Giuseppe Fiorelli, Enrico Stevens, Giovanni Pellegrini and Ettore Gabrici. The collection of material from Cuma is followed by a section dedicated to Naples. This contains material from the earliest Greek settlement of Parthenope, discovered in the necropolis of Pizzofalcone, and dating to somewhere between the 7th century and the 6th century B.C.; and the finds from the "new city" (Neapolis) which, according to legend, was founded around 475 B.C. by the inhabitants of the island of Ischia, which had been placed under the political control of Syracuse and the city of Cumae. Confirmation of what we know from literary sources is provided by the wealth of funerary artefacts from the necropolis of Castelcapuano, exhibited together with the more recent finds from the necropolis of Santa Teresa. This was excavated during the 19th century and most of its finds have been lost. There is plenty of evidence for cult activity in Neapolis; a magnificent votive deposit was found on the hill of Sant'Aniello in Caponapoli (on the site of the ancient acropolis), made up of over 700 votive terracottas that probably came from the Sanctuary of Demeter. Further evidence is provided by the statues of the Dioscuri from the temple of the Dioscuri in the *agora* (market place in the very heart of the city); the temple was restored at the start of the empire as a result of the growing imperial cult and later incorporated into the Church of St. Paolo Maggiore.

Lekythos vase from Cuma,
detail of a panther

## The House of Punta Chiarito

A recent and fruitful excavation has uncovered a small village of huts on the promontory of Punta Chiarito in the southern part of the island of Ischia. The huts date to the second half of the 8th century B.C. and were buried by a mudslide during the 6th century BC. This is an extraordinary discovery above all because of the exceptional state of preservation of the village due to a tragic fate that foreshadowed what would happen to nearby Pompeii. In one of the exhibition rooms of the Naples Museum, a hut from the village has been reconstructed to exemplify Greek domestic architecture in the first phase of the colony's life.

The house was oval in shape, with the entrance on one of the longer sides and a floor of beaten earth. Alongside the dry-stone walls were post holes used to insert the poles which held up the roof. The roof was tiled at the centre but was made of reeds and brushwood on the outer part. The spatial layout inside was as follows: a storage room for foodstuffs (situated just inside the entrance), a kitchen with a fireplace and a bedroom on the upper floor. The storage room mainly revealed large containers (amphorae and *pithoi*), locally produced and Greek and Etruscan imports, as well as cooking ware and fine wares which were also found throughout the house. A particular interesting discovery was an unfinished vase containing lumps of bronze which probably served as a precious metal for commercial exchanges, given that money was not yet used in this period. The numerous imported vases were almost all in some way connected to Greek banqueting ritual: a Laconian krater, Ionic cups, Corinthian kraters, bronze basins with a pearled border and strainers. Fishing gear (bronze fishhooks and lead weights for the nets), farming equipment (sickles, pickaxes), a few weapons (the tip of a spear and a sword), and loom-weights used for women's domestic activities, were all found in the kitchen near the hearth.

# first floor

## Magna Graecia

The section dedicated to Greek culture in the Bay of Naples and non-Hellenic cultures in Campania concludes with a display of material from the main sites of Magna Graecia. The Museum has acquired this material over the centuries as the result of frequently disorganized and unsupervised private excavations or due to the mania for private collections. The pieces in the Museum are unfortunately only a small part of what was found during these excavations. Artefacts were lost due to the lack of effective antiquities legislation and the sometimes willful negligence of court officials who were more interested in the finds from the excavations of the Vesuvian cities or the Phlegrean Fields. Another explanation for the loss of so much of the heritage of Magna Graecia was the great passion for "Etruscan vases" made famous by the rich Hamilton Collection, and for the fine Wedgwood porcelain that was inspired by it. It was during this period that large private collections were formed and later enlarged with the finds from excavations and clandestine markets. On occasion these collections found their way into the Royal Collections; the most important was the Santangelo Collection acquired by the Museum in 1865 through the efforts of Giuseppe Fiorelli. The establishment of provincial museums, an idea originally put forward in vain by Michele Arditi in 1808, and the creation of autonomous superintendencies, brought to an end this flow of material from Magna Grecia into the Naples Museum, hopefully ending once and for all one of the darkest periods of national archaeology.

Several of the groups acquired over the years by the Museum are of particular importance, such as the large collection of Apulian vases from Ruvo and Canosa, the Tarantine goldware found in the same tombs, the figured terracottas, the weapons, the funerary paintings, the coins and finally the inscriptions. These collections document the earliest scientific approaches to the history of Magna Grecia, putting an end to a tradition of humanistic studies embodied between the 16th and 18th centuries by scholars intent on exalting the cities of southern Italy.

82

Panathenaic amphora from Cuma,
detail with a discus-thrower

## The dancers of Ruvo

These famous paintings, which entered the Royal Collections of Naples in 1838, were discovered five years earlier in a tomb at Ruvo in Puglia with no grave goods other than a figured vase of exquisite workmanship. The damage caused to the frescoes during their discovery prevented their sale on the antiquarian market, but has also undoubtedly hindered full understanding of the monument. The walls of the chamber were divided horizontally in equal segments by a black band. The background of the lower section was yellow, while above, three bands, black, white and red, marked the limits of the painted area. Across the centre, on a white background, winds a procession of women. They are all depicted in profile and dressed in long chitons and bright, multi-coloured (ochre, red, blue and black) cloaks cover their heads too. The figures are moving to the right, with their hands interlinked, and each has a foot raised in a dance step. These female figures are accompanied by some boys who wear short white chitons and high black boots. They lead the movements of the women in the dance and provide the music, playing instruments such as a seven-stringed lyre. The scene depicts a very ancient funerary ritual, a *threnos*. This involved dances and choral laments performed while the body of the deceased was displayed and while the funerary procession proceeded to the tomb. The *chorus* of women holding hands brings to mind, on a mythological level, the merry dance that Theseus and the young Athenians performed in Crete to celebrate the death of the Minotaur. If, however, as in our case, it refers to a funerary context, they allude directly to the social and political prestige of the departed. Furthermore, the adoption of an Attic-inspired theme in an Apulian burial towards the end of the 5th century reflects the political events of those years, during which Athens collaborated with the indigenous centres of Puglia in order to stop the dangerous growth of Tarantum's power.

# first floor

## Ancient Pottery

The very rich pottery collection of the Museo Archeologico di Napoli (c. 8000 vessels) provides a remarkable selection of evidence for the pottery found in Campania, Greece and Magna Graecia. It covers a broad chronological span, from the 8th century BC to the Roman period. The collections includes examples of vessels produced in a number of traditions, including the Geometric to Corinthian periods; from the workshops of the East Greek world to Etruscan and Campanian bucchero, through Attic black- and red-figure vessels right down to the Italiot pottery of southern Italy, including the very famous, immense Apulian kraters of the 4th century BC; pottery from Campania and Lucania, and so-called Gnathian Ware, characterized by over-painted polychrome decoration. This collection made by the Bourbons, acquired in the 18th and 19th centuries and enhanced by material from contemporary excavations (at Paestum, Ruvo, Canosa, Nola, Nocera and Cuma), includes within it some of the most important ceramic collections of that time. These include the collection of Caroline Murat, that of the Vivenzio family (vessels from the *necropoleis* at Nola), that of Cuma (goods from the tombs of the Greek colony of *Kyme*), the Zoratti collection (vessels from Puglia and Basilicata), the Falconnet collection (from the Etruscan cemeteries of Canino), the very rich collection of the Santangelo family (wealthy collectors of the late 18th- early 19th century who acquired over a thousand examples, to the extent that the "Museo" Santangelo was considered a necessary stop-off point for scholars of archaeology passing through Naples in the 1800s) and, finally, the Stevens collection (from the cemeteries of Cuma) and the Spinelli collection (from the excavation of *Suessula*).

Vivenzio *hydria*, detail
with Priam killed by Neoptolemos

### Vivenzio *hydria*

This *hydria* belonged to the brothers Nicola and Pietro Vivenzio, famous tomb excavators and collectors of the 18th century. It presents one of the most famous representations of the *Ilioupersis* (sack of Troy), employing the red-figure technique on the upper parts of the vase and attributed to the "Kleophrades Painter". The vessel was widely appreciated from the time of its discovery. Its exceptional quality derives from the arrangement of its decorative scheme, as well as the narrative content of the scenes depicted, sometimes in overlapping planes. The scenes depicted are not just the usual ones connected with the fall of Troy, like the bloody depictions of slaughter (Priam killed by Neoptolemos, in the centre) and episodes focusing on violence and despair (Cassandra violated by Ajax at the cult statue of Athena) but also uncommon ones. These include the freeing of the elderly Etra (mother of Theseus), saved by her grandsons, the flight of Aeneas with Anchises and Ascanius, and the courage of the Trojan women face-to-face with their enemies. The vase, datable to c. 490-480 BC, was used as a cinerary urn, placed in a *dolium*. Inside the *hydria* were found, besides the remains of the deceased, five alabaster unguentaria and a gem engraved with an eagle with a snake in its talons.

### *Pronomos* **krater**

This vase, a masterpiece of Attic pottery production of the late 5th century BC, derives its fame from the exceptional quality of its decoration as well as the originality displayed in its iconography. The many characters depicted, set on two registers, can be identified from the Greek inscriptions with their names, written next to each figure. The principal decorated face of the vessel shows preparation for a performance of a satyr play with Dionysus and Ariadne as audience. They are surrounded by actors in costume, who hold painted masks in their hands. The krater is an exceptionally important piece of evidence because of the wealth of information it provides about satyr drama – about the costumes, the musicians and the characters involved in the spectacle. In the middle of the lower register is the character who gave his name to the vase and to its painter. Sitting on a stool is the flute-player *Pronomos*, whose name is known from written sources to have been that of a real Theban musician. The vessel can be dated to c. 400 BC, and comes from Ruvo, but given that it originates from a private collection (Ficco and Cervone), the original context in which it was found is unknown.

**Vase of the Persians**

This krater, discovered at Canosa in 1851, was one component of the grave goods in a large hypogeum (known as the Tomb of the Vase of Darius). It was found there with seven other vessels, all of large size and attributed to the same artisan. This is one of the most famous works of Italiot vase painting. It gets its name from the central character in the scene depicting the council held by the Persian king on the eve of the war against the Greeks. Darius, seated on a throne, sceptre in hand, listens to a messenger. Set around him, on two registers, are other characters: a court treasurer, (with a tablet in his hands), finely dressed court dignitaries and aged elders. In the upper register is an assembly of gods, with Zeus presiding, seated on a throne in the centre, reflecting the position of Darius. There is an amazonomachy (battle between Greeks and Amazons) on the neck of the vase, fitting in with the overall theme of the vessel. The female warriors represent barbarians in the Greek consciousness, particularly the Persians. Most scholars consider this painting to have been conceived as a depiction of a theatrical presentation, inspired by a tragedy called *The Persians*, written by Phrynichus. The body of the vase may be a symbolic representation of the theatre, with the chorus in the lower register, the proscenium in the centre, and a dais for the gods at the top. At any rate, the theme depicted on the vase relates to its function as a funerary item intended for the aristocracy of Canosa, probably men who fell fighting alongside Alexander the Molossian, the uncle of Alexander the Great. In fact these themes were taken up again and re-employed in the second half of the 4th century BC to present the ideology of power in the Macedonian court, with its emphasis on the exploits of Alexander the Great in combat against Darius III (Codomannus).

93

# first floor

## The Great Hall of the Sundial

The Great Hall of the Sundial is one of the most impressive roofed halls in Europe (54.80m long, 20.80m wide, 20.35m high). It was begun in 1612/1615 at the command of the viceroy don Pedro Fernando de Castro, and was intended to house the 'Studi' and the public library. The work continued thanks to Charles III, who wanted to unite the Farnese Library, which had become the property of the Bourbons, with the public library. In the reign of Ferdinand IV, in 1782, the Great Staircase and the Hall were restored as part of a project directed by the Roman architect Pompeo Schiantarelli. He reconstructed the floor with glazed bricks (the current polychrome marble floor dates to the 19th century) and replaced the old book cupboards with walnut shelving set off with gilded cornices and constructed on two levels. The vault was decorated with a magnificent fresco by the Neapolitan artist Pietro Bardellino, a work of art that celebrated the virtues of Ferdinand IV and his wife Maria Carolina of Austria as patrons of the arts. The paintings of the Genovese School that decorate the upper parts of the walls were dedicated to the celebration of the noble deeds of Alessandro Farnese, general of Charles V. Originally the tapestries depicting the Farnese victory at the battle of Pavia were displayed in the same location as these paintings – now they are in the Capodimonte Museum. The official opening of the library was in 1783, although work on the hall was to continue. It underwent its final major changes between 1790 and 1793, when there was a plan, proposed by the astronomer Giuseppe Casella, to install an astronomical observatory in the north-west corner. This project was abandoned more or less straight away, but the sundial on the floor that gives its name to the room was completed. It is 27 metres long, made up of a brass strip set between marble panels. On them are delicately presented medallions that show the twelve signs of the zodiac. The sundial still works, by means of a ray of light that shines into the room at midday through a hole that was made in the south-west corner of the room.

# first floor

## Vesuvian painting

The collection of paintings from Herculaneum and Pompeii is, in terms of quantity and quality, one of the most famous of the ancient world. The paintings were late arrivals to the Museum, brought there in the years immediately after the restoration and return of the Bourbons when the royal Palazzo degli Studi became the Royal Bourbon Museum. Until that time the paintings – ever increasing in number from the excavations of the Vesuvian cities – had been kept at Portici (1738-1826). The new arrangement of the paintings was inaugurated recently and presents the paintings of the Vesuvian cities within a chronological and art-historical framework. In the future the paintings will be arranged in large thematic sections (as already done in the rooms relating to the Temple of Isis, to exemplify a cult), illustrating subjects such as the house, banquet, spectacles and public buildings. In this scheme the examples of Italiot and Magna Grecia tomb paintings will be given their rightful places within an appropriate section. With the exception of the paintings of the so-called First Style (which were left in the houses because they are plain), the Naples collection documents the evolution of Roman pictorial styles from the late Republic to the Empire, from the theatrical scenes of the Villa of Publius Fannio Synistor at Boscoreale, to the mythological or landscape paintings which were so popular at the beginning of the Empire. The Fourth Style section is particularly rich. These paintings date back to the final phase of the Vesuvian cities. Good examples are the grand paintings found in the Basilica of Herculaneum which celebrate the foundation myths and the illustrious genealogies of the city; the picture gallery inspired by Homeric subjects found in the House of the Tragic Poet; the fine friezes of cupids at work from the House of the Deer of Herculaneum; and the small, whimsical, still-life paintings found in Pompeian homes.

Silenus, from the Villa of Cicero, Pompeii

## Roman painting and the Pompeian 'styles'

"The ancients who began the fashion for wall decorations at first imitated the variegated appearance and arrangement of marbled stucco, and subsequently various combinations of wreaths, small buds and leaves. Later on, they began to imitate the shapes of buildings, protruding columns and pediments, and to paint tragic, comic and satirical scenic backgrounds in open spaces such as exedrae, due to their width. Decorations depicting various landscapes according to the characteristics of the specific area were painted in covered walkways, due to their great length. There are paintings of ports, promontories, beaches, rivers, streams, straits, sanctuaries, sacred groves, mountains, flocks of sheep, shepherds, and some use *megalographia* (life-sized figures) instead of statues, portraits of divinities, even narration in a series of mythological scenes, such as the battles fought at Troy or the locations of the wanderings of Ulysses and decorative elements which, in the same way as these, have been created by nature. These figurative subjects which were copies of real elements are today frowned upon due to the spread of a new and depraved style. The walls are painted with monstrosities instead of precise depictions that conform to well-defined objects: instead of columns there are reeds; instead of pediments there are ornamental designs with curled and spiral leaves; there are candelabras bearing images of temples with delicate flowers poking through the pediments, as well as roots coming up through the volutes and in the centre for no reason, there are seated figures; small stems bearing figures divided into two halves, one with a human head and the other with an animal head. But these figures do not exist, they cannot exist, they have never existed ... and yet, people see these deceptions and, instead of criticizing them, are delighted, without reflecting if they could possibly exist in reality or not."

This is what Vitruvius (VII.5.1ff.) wrote in regard to ancient pictorial styles, from the end of the 2nd century B.C. to the Augustan age. This well-known passage has influenced all the specialized studies of modern times, and is the basis of the chronological division of the four Pompeian styles.

**FIRST STYLE** Also known as the "encrustation" or "structural" style, the painted polychrome stucco panels of First Style imitate the isodomic structure of blocks of marble. It is of Greek origin and was used frequently throughout the 2nd century BC.

**SECOND STYLE** Also known as the "architectural" style, Second Style is characterized by the depiction of realistic architecture across the walls, which creates a perspective effect within the room. The walls are divided into zones: the socle, middle zone with architectural elements, and upper zone with fake porticoes, colonnaded rooms and theatrical backdrops. The style remained in use throughout the 1st century BC until the beginning of the imperial period (from 90/80 BC to the end of the century).

**THIRD STYLE** Also known as the "ornamental" style, Third Style abandons the fake perspectives of the Second style and introduces decorative systems (thin columns, candelabras) organized according to the same scheme (dado, middle zone and upper zone) and framing a central area which contained mythological scenes. Typical of the Augustan age, the style was used until the first half of the 1st century AD (from 15 BC to AD 45).

**FOURTH STYLE** Also known as the "fantastic" style, Fourth Style re-introduces the architectural elements of the Second Style in compositions which are far richer and more complex; on the panels of the middle zone, which are framed by characteristic 'carpet' borders, there are isolated figures or mythological scenes. This style was developed from the middle of the 1st century AD onwards (from AD 45-AD 79).

## Flora

The figure of a young girl is painted on a green background, her back turned to the viewer and intent on collecting white flowers from a small tree. Using her right hand, she places the flowers in a *kalathos* held in her left hand. The young girl wears a yellow tunic and her hair is gathered at the nape in a *chignon,* and adorned with a diadem. This subject was inspired by paintings of the 4th century BC and was found together with three other frescos of similar subject depicting Leda (again, on a green background), Medea and Diana (on a blue background). These panels were located in the middle zone of the walls of a *cubiculum* in the Villa Arianna at Stabia. It is unclear whether this figure is human or divine, a nymph, Flora or Persephone. Her identification as a nymph is suggested by a passage by Ovid, which describes the nymph as the one who 'rules over everything that flowers' (Ovid, *Fasti* V.20).

### Hercules and Telephus

This painting from the Basilica of Herculaneum is a copy of the famous painting, *Hercules turning*, by Apelles, which Pliny says was located in the Roman temple of Diana on the Aventine Hill. The painting depicts the Greek hero watching the remarkable scene of his small son Telephus being suckled by a doe. A seated personification of Arcadia holding a lush basket of fruit, the eagle of Zeus Olympus and the lion of Nemea complete the scene. This episode was also represented on the altar of Pergamon, highlighting the mythical origins of that city and the Attalid dynasty and has very strong connections with the Roman legend of the she-wolf and the founder-twins. This can be explained by the common Trojan origins of both peoples (the Romans and the Pergamenes). This legend was disseminated from the start of the 2nd century BC, as shown by the ancient decoration of the Temple of Apollo at Cyzicus (representing Romulus and Remus) and panels from Campania of later date, depicting the myths of Telephus and the twin founders of Rome.

The Basilica of Herculaneum was also decorated with other great mythological scenes, such as Theseus the liberator, Achilles and Chiron, Marsyas and Olympus. The choice of subject matter for the decoration of the Basilica is connected both to the myths regarding the foundation of this Vesuvian city that had elected Hercules as its eponymous hero, and also to the policy of religious restoration promoted by the Flavian emperors, concentrating on themes relating to the origins of Rome. The legend of Hercules' son also inspired the neo-Attic relief, known as the relief of Telephus, found in a house in Herculaneum and now in the Naples Museum.

## Achilles and Chiron

The large podium behind Chiron and Achilles locates this scene in an architectural context and gives an air of isolation to the two characters, in a manner that recalls the famous marble groups displayed at Rome inside the *Saepta Julia*. The elderly Centaur wears an animal skin over his shoulder, as if to emphasis his wild nature, which is also brought to mind by his piercing eyes. He has an expression of intense concentration on his face in comparison to that of the young man whom he is teaching to play the lyre. Achilles was taught music by the wisest of the centaurs, who was also master of the hunt, ethics, the arts of war, and medicine. This painting belongs at the end of a pictorial cycle depicting the education given at different stages of life; here it depicts the education of *iuvenes* (young men).

**Europa on the bull**

This Fourth Style painting decorated the wall of a room in the House of Jason. It depicts the first scene in the myth of Europa, who was kidnapped and taken to Crete by Zeus, who had turned himself into a bull, and gave birth to Minos, Rhadamanthus and Sarpedon. The scene derives from a Hellenistic model, as seen from the pyramidal structure of the group, the point of which coincides with the top of a column. The smooth column is located at the centre of the scene along with an an oak tree, which was sacred to Zeus; in the background is a rocky landscape, with trees, shrubs and stepped rocks. The female figures are drawn from models of different origins, which the artist uses skillfully. The painting revises somewhat the myth of the kidnap of Europa by Zeus; in the classical version Zeus immediately took the girl by sea to the island of Crete.

## Perseus and Andromeda

The liberation of Andromeda by Perseus is one of the most commonly painted subjects in antiquity. It symbolized the *virtus* of the hero, tested in his battle with the sea monster, and the chastity of the promised young bride. This Fourth Style fresco depicts the hero in the act of freeing the young girl, having killed the monster that lies on its back on the ground. It is the largest fresco of this subject to have been found and appears to be the closest imitation of the work of *Nikias*, the Athenian painter of the late Classical period whose works were copied by the Romans. In addition, while the Third Style paintings of this subject depict a great number of episodes and the presence of minor mythological characters (such as Cassiopea and Cephaus), later versions have only the two main protagonists, Perseus and Andromeda, a reference to their future together.

## Theseus the liberator

This painting decorated the exedra of the House of Gavius Rufus. Its subject derives from the epilogue of the myth of Theseus, who freed the young Athenians from the tribute imposed by the Cretans that demanded that every year seven boys and seven girls should be sent as an offering to the Minotaur. The monster lies dead on the ground, to the left. The hero is depicted at the centre of the field, posed like a statue. The painting was inspired by a famous 4th century BC work, another copy of which existed in the Basilica of Herculaneum. The arrangement of the walls in the background may well derive from the Greek original, and serve to highlight the stationary figure of the hero. The group on the right of Cretan women, who have come to see the dead body of the monster, is considered to be a Roman addition.

## The sacrifice of Iphigenia

This large Fourth Style fresco depicts an episode that is also known as *Iphigenia at Aulis.* In the centre Agamemnon's daughter is led to the sacrificial altar by Ulysses and Diomedes (or Achilles). On the left, Agamemnon, entirely veiled, with his face hidden by a hand. Pliny says that the painter rendered the king like this because he was unable to depict his grief. To the right is Calchas, the Argive priest, who holds in his hand the sacrificial instruments. There are two female busts emerging from the clouds in the upper part of the panel; they are Artemis and a nymph who leads a stag, which will be substituted for the young girl in the sacrifice. The fresco illustrates a classical composition known to us from ancient literary sources as the work of the painter *Timanthes*, but its structure lacks homogeneity: the series of figures seems to be images taken from different sources. Agamemnon and Calchas, for example, are much greater in stature than Ulysses and his companion. The crude composition is particularly evidence in the central group, in the strange way in which the girl is held and in her unusual pose. In addition, only the figure of Agamemnon is represented, while we know from the literary sources that in the original painting Menelaus was also depicted (although he is nowhere to be seen here), and that Iphigenia stood before the altar.

### *Terentius* **Neo and his wife**

This Fourth Style fresco of the late Neronian period is one of the most famous paintings in the Museum. It was found on the rear wall of the House of Terentius Neo, positioned in such as way that it could be seen by anyone who passed by in the atrium. It is only recently that the portrait has been convincingly identified as that of the baker Terentius Neo, the owner of the house. Previously it was thought to depict Paquius Proculus, whose name appears in an inscription on the external façade of the house. The husband and wife are portrayed as people of means, cultured and fashionable. The woman wears a red cloak, a pearl necklace with golden pendent and pearl earrings. Her hair is styled fashionably, parted at the centre and gathered at the nape, in the typical style of the Neronian period. She holds a wax tablet and a stylus, assuming the same pose seen in the portrait of the so-called Sappho. The baker wears a white today that reveals his magisterial dignity, and he holds up a papyrus roll. Their facial features have been rendered faithfully by the painter and betray their provincial origin (they were probably from Samnium). This clashes somewhat with the cultured tone that their gestures and attributes attempt to establish.

## Medallion with portrait bust, the so-called Sappho

This medallion was found in June 1760 and is one of the most famous frescoes in the Museum. The girl is depicting holding a polyptych made up of four wax tablets in her left hand and, in her right, a stylus that she holds to her lips with an air of reflection. The panel was paired with a male portrait. The composition follows a common scheme, employed, for example, in the portrait of *Terentius Neo*. In this example, in fact, the face is presented without any particular intention of depicting a real individual, something that also excludes the possibility of identifying the woman as the famous Greek poetess from which the painting derives its name. More likely the artist just wished to depict someone cultured, of high social status (implied by the gold jewellery and the hair net, in fashion in the reign of Nero). Painted medallions of this kind typically were used as ornaments in reception rooms, such as *triclinia* and *tablina*, and only occasionally depicted real individuals.

**Girls playing with knuckle-bones**

Painted on marble, this panel is probably a Neo-Attic revision of a Greek original (perhaps by Zeuxis). This is suggested by the signature in the top left corner, where the following can be read: *Alexandros Athenaios egrapse* (the Athenian Alexander painted this). The names in capital letters are written next to each figure: *Letò* (Latona), *Niobe* (Niobe), *Foibe* (Phoebe), *Aglaia* (Agles) e *Ileara* (Hilearia). The scene depicts the moment immediately before the slaughter of the daughters of Niobe (planned by Latona and executed by her children, Apollo and Artemis), who is to be punished for boasting that she is the most fertile of mothers. In the foreground the daughters are playing with knucklebones; their mother is pushed by Phoebe towards Latona, who turns away. The inclusion of the names next to the characters can be attributed to the archaizing fashion of the Augustan period. The painting (and nine similar ones kept at the Museum) is usually referred to as a monochrome marble, since to the naked eye only the ochre outline of the scene is now visible. However, recent tests have shown that other colours were used: the clothes were pink and yellow, the sandals red and black, the hair black, and different shades of colour were used to give the figures depth.

## Riot between Pompeians and Nucerians

This painting comes from the peristyle of a house. It shows the riot involving Pompeians and Nucerians that broke out at games in the amphitheatre in Pompeii in AD 59. In the aftermath of this riot, the amphitheatre was closed for ten years (Tacitus, *Annals* 14.17). The painting has no obvious antecedents, and one can only suggest that it reflects the triumphal painting of the Republican period known only from descriptions by ancient writers and with reference to the relief friezes of spiral columns in the imperial period. Common features include the care with which the details are rendered, in a realistic manner, the absence of perspective and the birds-eye view. The fresco depicts they crucial moment of the riot as the confrontation floods down the steps of the amphitheatre into the city beyond, the area close to the city walls and the palaestra – one can even see the *natatio* (swimming-pool) inside the latter. The amphitheatre stands out in the centre of the image. It is possible to make out the access stairs and the *velarium* suspended above the amphitheatre. On the inside there are figures visible fighting on the stepped seating. The lower part of the panel is filled by the stalls of itinerant traders and small trees that provide some shade from the heat of the sun. All the figures are the same size, with no regard to perspective or illusionism, both of which are such important elements of Hellenistic painting.

**Bacchus and Vesuvius**

This is a fourth style fresco that decorated the *lararium* in a service atrium of the House of the Centenary at Pompeii, along with another painting with scenes showing *lares* (household gods). Dionysus/Bacchus is shown on the left, his body (apart from his face and hands) covered completely by huge grapes. He holds his usual attributes – the *thyrsus* and *kantharos* – in his hands. To the right is a single tall mountain, its slopes covered in vines. It is much-debated whether we should identify this mountain as Vesuvius (with a single peak, before the AD 79 eruption), or as Mount Nysa, where Dionysus grew up. Motifs such as the hanging garlands with their ribbons, the birds and the snake crawling towards the altar with an egg are part of a common repertoire of decoration found on *lararia*.

### *Megalographia* **from the Villa of Publius Fannius Synistor at Boscoreale**

The Naples Museum preserves some of the sumptuous painted decoration of this villa, which constitutes one of the best preserved examples of the Second Style. One part, from the decorative scheme of the *triclinium,* is centred on a monumental doorway with with panelled shutters, culminating in a frieze depicting hunting scenes which evoke the Macedonian tombs of the Hellenistic age. Another section forms part of the decoration of an *oecus,* and constitutes an example of the famous form of composition known as *megalographia* (depiction of large-scale figures), here portraying historical subjects. The painted panels are framed by monumental columns and crowned with a doric frieze with a perspective rendering of a colonnade behind. The panels show two figures seated opposite one other; the figure in the foreground, wearing a Persian headdress, may be a personification of Persia or Asia, or of queen Phila, mother of Antigonus Gonatas. Also uncertain is the identification of the second figure, with a long spear (*sarissa*), *kausia* (the distinctive Macedonian headgear, held on by a regal headband) and a large shield with an eight-pointed star in the centre. It may be a depiction of a Hellenistic ruler (Antigonus Gonatas, Antigonus Doson or Demetrius Poliorcetes) or an allegorical depiction of Macedonia. The old man leaning on a stick, looking towards the seated figures, is probably to be identified as a philosopher or a prophetic sage. This grand fresco is generally considered to be a copy of a famous painting, probably itself a wall-painting, that actually existed once in a public building or Macedonian palace.

## Landscape Paintings

"We must give credit to Studius, who lived during the Augustan age and was the first to invent the grace-ful style of painting walls with images of country homes, ports, landscape themes, sacred groves, woods, hills, fish ponds, canals, rivers, beaches, according to the wishes of each patron. In each of these paint-ings, he included various figures of people who are either walking or navigating, or travelling towards their villa by land, donkey or cart, or fishing or hunting or even gathering grapes. Among the subjects he painted, there are also noble country homes which can be reached by crossing a marsh, and women car-ried by hired hands, turning on the shoulders of the trembling porters, as well as many other similar re-finements represented with exquisite skill. The same painter began painting maritime cities on external walls, beautiful works of art that cost very little" (Pliny the Elder, *Natural History*, 35.116-117). Landscape scenery, almost always of a sacred nature, became popular in Third Style paintings, as seen in contem-porary reliefs, exemplifying the climate of peace and prosperity established with the coming of the new era and spread by court poetry (Virgil, Propertius). It is with the popularity of the panel painting (that is, Third and Fourth Style painting) that landscapes become the backdrop to mythological scenes that take place in the open air. Rivers, rocks, woods outnumber the human figures; villas on land or by the sea, ru-ral shrines, river and ocean vistas with harbours are depicted from above. Suspended from pilasters and candelabra or painted in the socle, these landscapes are as important as the central panel painting. They are almost always fantasy landscapes, frequently Nilotic in theme, stylized and escapist in nature.

## Yellow monocrome

This is a rural landscape depicting a hill along with a stretch of water, a sanctuary with columns and a statue on a tall column, leaning on a long staff, perhaps a representation of Poseidon. The scene is completed by a group of worshippers near the sanctuary, a traveler crossing the bridge and a fisherman. On the mountains in the background, there are buildings that are depicted in more faded tones than the individuals depicted in the foreground. The technique of painting with a limited palette (or even a single colour) that contrasts with the colour of the wall was defined as *monochromatos* by Pliny (*Natural History* 35.15). It was much-liked, and used on second style walls in houses and villas in the Vesuvian region and beyond, particularly in depicting panels, architectural elements or mythological subjects. The genre of monochrome painting was considered particularly appropriate for sacro-idyllic landscapes like this one, with representations of "ports, promontories, beaches, rivers, streams, straits, sanctuaries, sacred groves, mountains, flocks of sheep and shepherds" (Vitruvius 7.5.2).

## Garden Paintings

Next to royal vestibules, atriums and peristyles, the garden was one of the features that Vitruvius (VI, 7, 10) considered essential in the homes of people who held public appointments. The ancient literary sources (and to a lesser extent the archaeological ones) demonstrate that, from the late Republic onwards, sacred groves (*silvae*) and covered walkways (*ambulationes*), lush with exotic plants and ornaments, enriched city dwellings as previously they had done suburban villas. So much so that Cicero, after restoring his house on the Palatine Hill, no longer felt the need go out into the country. This was a fashion that developed from the magnificent residences of Hellenistic princes and the successors of Alexander. At the same time, the custom became popular of painting gardens on the walls of living rooms or on the rear walls of open spaces. They were characterized by evergreen plants in perpetual bloom, inhabited by birds and enriched by sculptures which reflected, as did the royal gardens, social prestige and the need of the master of the house to show off. This genre, which may have been used first in the subterranean hall of the Villa of Livia at Prima Porta in Rome (today housed in the National Museum of Rome in the Palazzo Massimo alle Terme), was extremely popular, as can be seen from the examples from the Vesuvian cities. These range from the pictures of *horti* found on the Third Style walls to the *megalographia* with exotic animals of later paintings.

## Still Lives

In the ancient world still-lives were never became a genre of painting in their own right because the subjects they depicted were things of little importance, to the point of being distasteful. The oldest still-lives are those with baskets, hampers with fruit and vases; they are mere accessories within larger compositions, found with works of extraordinary quality that remind one of the anecdotes told by Pliny about birds that attempted to peck the grapes in a bunch painted by Zeuxis. In Roman painting still-lives are found between the end of the 2nd and beginning of the 1st century BC, in Second Style paintings at a time when 'villa life' became popular. Among Second Style paintings can be seen small panels (*pinakes*) with frames and windows with depictions of fruit, food (hard and soft cheese, eggs, bread), live animals or animals ready to be cooked, glass and silver vessels, even coins and writing implements. Vitruvius (VI. 7. 4) explains that the small still-life paintings derive from a Greek tradition of offering chickens, eggs, vegetables, fruits and other agricultural products to one's guests the day after a dinner invitation. This is why the term *xenia* (guest gifts) is applied to them. Still-lives can be located in the central parts of walls, in the zone usually reserved for painted mythological or narrative scenes, and it is unsurprising that they are found in dinning rooms (*triclinia*) or in rooms for entertainment (*oeci*). They are more rarely found in passage ways such as the porticoes of peristyles.

Pliny the Elder records an artist from the end of the 4th century B.C. by the name of Pireikos who, "though he was second to none as far as art was concerned, must be distinguished because although he always painted humble subjects, he nonetheless attained glory in the field of humility. He painted barbers and shoemakers, donkeys, food and the like, and for this reason he was called *rhyparographos*. On the other hand, he demonstrated his ability and determination with these subjects and his works were sold at a higher price than the greater works of many others" (*Natural History*, 35, 112).

This type of painting was later copied by Poxis, a Greek coraplaster, perhaps from Magnesia on the Menander, who was active in Rome during the late Republican period. Marcus Varro recounts having met and admired him for his paintings of fruit, grapes and fish, painted in such a realistic way that they could not be distinguished from the originals (Pliny the Elder, *Natural History*, 35.155).

The small panels located in the upper parts of walls and the isolated motifs in architectural settings of Second Style paintings continue in the subsequent Style. In the Third Style these panels were initially miniature and found on columns, in socles and on predelle; later they became bigger, substituting the mythological panels at the centre of Fourth Style walls.

## Fresco with still life

The three small panels from the House of the Stags at Herculaneum highlight the extraordinary harmony of the decorative cycle of this house, which is characterized by splendid still-lives of the Fourth Style. The first panel on the left depicted a pair of fish on a table, dangling over a lower shelf; on the right the stone of a split peach can be seen. On the lower shelf there is a glass container, half full of water. This subject is repeated in the panel to the right. Here the central composition also ranges over two shelves and focuses on the colour contrast between a glass *kantharos* that is full of red wine and a silver tray that holds plums, dried figs and dates among which can be seen two coins of gold and silver. On the lower shelf there are another two dates and beneath them a dried fig and a date. Martial (*Xenia* VIII.33) tells us that offerings of money and dates and the depictions of dried winter fruits symbolize the particular gift that clients would give to their *patroni* at the New Year.

# first floor

## The Sanctuary of Isis at Pompeii

In line with modern conceptions about how a museum of antiquities should be organized, the decoration of the Temple of Isis at Pompeii has been organized according to the original contexts of the finds. The success of this achievement is due to the wealth of documentation made when the temple was discovered during the early years of the Bourbon excavations (between 1764-1766). The sanctuary was built towards the end of the 2nd century B.C. in the theatre quarter of Pompeii, close to the Temple of Aesculapius and the Temple of Minerva which, at this time, was enclosed and provided with an elegant *tholos* and propylaeum at the entrance. The damage caused by the earthquake of AD 62 required the complete reconstruction of the building. This was financed by Numerius Popidius Ampliatus in the name of his six-year-old son Celsinus, and recorded in a dedicatory inscription placed over the main entrance. The temple was enclosed by a portico which became what Vitruvius describes as a 'Rhodian peristyle'. The splendid, brightly-coloured Fourth Style decoration on the rear wall has red panels with Isiac scenes and small landscapes and architecture which alternate with panels with landscapes scenes and imaginary architecture. An elegant black frieze runs along the top border with gyrals and objects related to the cult of Isis; above are panels with still lives, which allude to the sacrifices offered in honour of the goddess. The actual temple is located in the centre of the courtyard, a tetrastyle prostyle on a high podium. The interior and exterior walls of the cella are completely faced with white stucco that imitates *opus quadratum*. A brick platform on the rear wall held the cult statues of Isis and Osiris. Two other niches were found on either side of the entrance, which may have contained the statues of Harpocrates and Anubis to whom two altars in the courtyard were dedicated. There were many altars with dedicatory inscriptions in the courtyard, and also a small, enclosed subterranean room used for purification ceremonies, known as the *purgatorium*. The enclosure-wall was richly decorated with paintings and stuccoes depicting the love between Mars and Venus, and Perseus and Andromeda. The *ekklesiasterion* and the real *sacrarium* were located on the east side of the courtyard. The *ekklesiasterion* was a room used for meetings and banquets, and its painted decoration was very fine, including the famous paintings of the myths of Io arriving in Canopos and the liberation of Argus from captivity. The sculpture found in the temple included a bronze herm of Norbanus Sorex from the portico, dating to the early Augustan age; an archaic-style statue of Isis which was a votive offering by Lucius Caecilius Phoebus, dating to the reign of the emperor Claudius; the head of the goddess found near the entrance to the *ekklesiasterion*; and, finally, two female portraits of early Imperial date.

Painting of Io at Canopos

# first floor

## The model of Pompeii

This scale model was commissioned by Giuseppe Fiorelli and largely made between 1861 and 1864 by Felice Padiglioni. It reproduces at a scale of 1:100 the buildings of Pompeii that were excavated before 1879. The model belongs to a highly skilled craft tradition, brought to the Royal Bourbon Museum by Domenico Padiglione (Felice's father) who was responsible for making the wood and cork models of the temples of Paestum, the Colosseum of Rome and several other Pompeian buildings, all originally displayed in a special room in the Naples Picture Gallery. The model of Pompeii measures 8 x 5m; only the amphitheatre, the *insula occidentalis* and *insula* 2 of *region* VIII are missing, and obviously all the buildings brought to light by excavations since the model was made. The model of Pompeii has recently undergone a careful and extensive restoration. The materials used in its construction are plywood (for the base of the buildings and the streets); cork (for the walls of the buildings) cut to reproduce the different ancient building techniques; plaster; and paper (for the paintings and the floors). Its importance as historical documentation is clear, above all with regard to the wall and floor decoration which is rendered with extraordinary delicacy and precision.

# Furnishings in the Vesuvian cities

In the past as today, the archaeological excavations of the Vesuvian cities are an extraordinary source of knowledge about all aspects of daily life in Roman republican and imperial society. Here we have the architecture of the houses, their floor and wall decoration, furnishings and household objects. A magnificent array of household furnishings can be seen in the east wing of the first floor, including precious silver accessories, fine ceramic tableware, personal ornaments, gladiatorial equipment, glass vases, small and large bronze decorative sculptures, kitchen utensils and table vessels, and ceramic lararium statuettes. The Hellenisation of fashions, and the advent of Asian *luxuria* in Roman houses in the Republic period influenced the architectural transformation of the classical atrium house, leading to innovations such as "high regal vestibules, wide atriums and peristyles, extremely large gardens and porticoes, as well as libraries, picture galleries and basilicas which were as magnificent as the public ones" (Vitruvius, VI.5.2). The decorative arts and tablewares were also influenced; the simple and modest household items of ancient times were exchanged for fine and precious silver table services which the nobles loved to flaunt at their feasts and banquets as a sign of their social and economic status. Antique pieces were particularly sought after, including the cups depicting bucolic scenes found among the treasures of the House of Menander, and the bronze *hydria* from the Classical period used as a fountain-head in the Pompeian house of Julius Polybius. The decorative designs of the furnishings of the *triclinia* and the living rooms were inspired by Greek mythology, and the sculptures placed as ornaments in the homes and gardens were copied from Classical and Hellenistic prototypes. A lampstand in the form of a statue was found in the Pompeian House of the Lyre-Player, thought to have been inspired by an Apollo made by the master Pheidias. It is a prime example of a fashion criticized by contemporary moralists of using "gold statues of young men holding lit torches with their right hand in order to illuminate nocturnal orgies" (Lucretius, *The Nature of Things*, II.20ff). The start of the imperial period saw new figurative themes, reactions to the new ideology that celebrated the emperor and his family, that spread to all areas of public and private life. Even the family *lararium* was affected, as can be seen in the terracotta group representing Aeneas in flight from Troy with the eldery Anchises and the young Ascanius. This was the official symbol chosen by Augustus to illustrate the Trojan origins of the Julian family; here it was used as a sign of private devotion to the ideas and figureheads of official religion.

## The silver from the House of Menander

The House of Menander is named after the wall-painting of the Greek comic playwright Menander. A magnificent silver hoard was found in this house and is today displayed in the Naples Museum. It is made up of 118 pieces, several of which were quite old and had been restored. The vessels were found at the bottom of a wooden case that had been placed in the cellar during restoration work that was taking place in the house as a result of the earthquake of AD 62. They had been wrapped in pieces of cloth and wool to protect them. The upper part of the case contained the family jewels (earrings, necklaces, gold bracelets and rings set with precious stones), and a hoard of gold and silver coins amounting to 1,432 *sestertii*. Among the silverware were several valuable cups embossed with scenes of the myths (the love of Mars and Venus; the labours of Hercules; Dionysus and his entourage), or with traditional Hellenistic landscapes (these last ones the work of the Greek *argentarius* Apelles). The owner of this luxurious home, or at least its last owner, is thought to be Quintus Poppaeus, a well-known tile-maker related to Poppaea Augusta, the second wife of Nero, who owned the Villa of Oplontis.

## Amphoretta with grape-harvest scene, the so-called Blue Vase

This is a vase decorated by the cameo-glass technique, and shaped – in harmony with its theme – as a wine amphora. The technique used to make it involves the application of a layer of white vitreous paste to parts of a blue glass base, here creating figures involved in a Dionysiac-themed grape-harvest. The scene is framed by Dionysiac masks from which descend grapevines, enlivened by birds; at the centre are joyous figures of cupids, who are either pressing grapes, banqueting or playing the flute and the syrinx. The same technique was used for the two panels depicting Dionysian scenes which probably belonged to the decoration of a triclinium bed in the Pompeian House of Fabius Rufus, now in the Museum of Naples. It is said that the Blue Vase was found in a tomb in the Herculaneum Gate necropolis of Pompeii in the presence of none other than King Ferdinand II.

**Cup made of rock crystal**

This deep cup is made of rock crystal, and has vertical handles and distinctive rich vegetal decoration, depicting branches with foliage. The shape of this *skyphos* reflects that of other such vessels made of silver, and allows us to date it to the reign of Augustus. It is one of the largest known objects in this material. It is made of a colourless and transparent quartz, often used in antiquity both for jewellery and to make small objects such as trinkets or amulets. The cup was found in a tomb, near Santa Maria Capua Vetere.

**Glass panel with portrait**

This is a convex glass panel, probably part of a double medallion, and mounted on a modern silver stand. A male portrait is depicted on a white background. This is certainly a masterpiece produced by a workshop of Alexandrian craftsmen active in Campania, as the discovery of two similar pieces in Naples and Cuma suggests.

## 'Millefiori' glass cup

Polychrome vases in the styles known as 'sprinkled', 'millefiori', 'golden ribbon' and 'pseudo-murrhine' were inherited from the eastern and Hellenistic world and enthusiastically copied. They were very popular in the Roman world in the early years of glass production. The 'pseudo-murrhine' vases enjoyed great favour due to their lively colours that imitate 'murrhine' vases of precious stone. Vases of this type, however, are exceptional. In Pompeii and the other Vesuvian cities good quality monochrome glass is the norm. This cup, part of a set of luxury tableware, is decorated in tones of white, yellow and blue, with symmetrical fish-spine motifs.

## *Skyphos* depicting Egyptianizing subjects

This deep *skyphos* was hollowed out of a single block of obsidian. Both the style and the subject matter of the decoration are Egyptianizing in character. Small coloured stone inserts have been set into locating holes made in the surface of the vessel, and overlaid with thin gold sheet. At the centre of the scene is a shrine, its pediment decorated with a Sun disc and two *urei* (cobras). Between the columns of the shrine is an Apis Bull, and behind it Horus, the falcon god. The worshippers are shown with frontal heads and profile legs, heads and arms, while the *pastophoroi* are kneeling on two tables. This cup, of Alexandrian manufacture, must serve to represent many such vessels that existed once, and provides us with exceptional evidence, both of the use of valuable materials and of such refined craftsmanship.

# first floor

## Gladiatorial games

The new lay-out of the museum in 2009 displayed to the public (on the first floor, in rooms next to the Hall of the Sundial) a selection of items relating to gladiatorial games in the Roman world. A remarkable selection of bronze weapons and equipment was discovered in the 18th century in the quadriporticus behind the theatre at Pompeii, a structure identified on that basis as the Gladiatorial Barracks. It included helmets, greaves, shields, spears and daggers, all richly decorated in relief. Gladiatorial games (*ludi*) took place in the amphitheatre. The amphitheatre at Pompeii, dated to 70 BC, is the oldest example completely preserved, and could accommodate c. 20,000 spectators. The relevant literary and epigraphic sources refer to certain types of gladiator, but it is not always possible to attribute particular names assigned to these types to particular types of dress and armament known from visual depictions and archaeological evidence. The oldest types seem to have derived their titles and armament from traditional enemies of the Romans. These included the *samnes* (Samnite), *traex* (Thracian) and *murmillo* (Samnite). Among the best-known types of gladiator there is also the *retiarius*, who took his name from the light net that he used to parry his enemy. His offensive weapons were the trident and dagger, and the only armour he wore was an arm-guard on his left, a shoulder-guard (*galerus*) and his broad belt.

### Gladiator's helmet

This is a bronze helmet with a brim that curves down towards the back and has a visor with grille. On the sides of the helmet's crown and on the *crista* there are small holes that were used to hold feathers and the horse hair of the crest. The crown is decorated in relief with a personification of Roma victorious, wearing amazon dress. She is shown between two kneeling male barbarians wearing tunic, trousers and cloak who are holding out a standard. To the sides are two standing prisoners (a man and a woman) with their hands tied behind their backs, along with heaps of weapons and trophies (breastplates, shields, spears and greaves) borne by two Victories. Under the brim there are two scenes. On one side there is a gigantomachy, with Minerva in the act of spearing a Giant (Pallas). On the other there is a Silenus, two masks and dionysiac symbols. This type of helmet was mostly used by a *hoplomachos* or by a *myrmillo*. The initials on the rim probably relate to the name of the craftsman or that of the helmet's owner. This example comes from the quadriporticus of the theatre at Pompeii, and can be dated to the Neronian or Flavian period.

### Gladiatorial shield

A circular bronze gladiatorial shield decorated at its centre with motifs in relief picked out in copper and silver (olive leaves, lines) around a medallion with the head of Medusa. A bronze strap for the arm is located on the inside. This example can be dated to the 1st century AD and was found in the Quadriporticus of the Theatres of Pompeii.

**133**

## Bibliography

A. Ruesch, *Guida illustrata del Museo Nazionale di Napoli,* Naples 1908.

O. Elia, *Pitture murali e mosaici nel Museo Nazionale di Napoli,* Rome 1932.

L. Breglia, *Catalogo delle oreficerie del Museo Nazionale di Napoli,* Naples 1941.

R. Siviero, *Gli ori e le ambre del Museo Nazionale di Napoli,* Naples 1954.

A. de Franciscis, *Il Museo Nazionale di Napoli*, Cava dei Tirreni-Naples 1963.

*Da Palazzo degli Studi a Museo Archeologico*, exhibition catalogue (Naples, Museo Archeologico Nazionale) Naples 1977.

*La collezione egiziana del Museo Archeologico Nazionale di Napoli,* Naples 1989.

M. Borriello, R. Cantilena (*et alii*), *Le collezioni del Museo Nazionale di Napoli,* 2 vols., Rome 1986 e 1989.

*Alla ricerca di Iside. Analisi, studi e restauri dell'Iseo pompeiano nel Museo di Napoli,* Naples 1992.

S. De Caro, *Il Museo Archeologico Nazionale di Napoli,* Naples 1994.

C. Gasparri, *Le gemme Farnese,* Naples 1994.

M. Borriello, S. De Caro, *La Magna Grecia nelle collezioni del Museo Archeologico di Napoli,* exhibition catalogue (Naples, Museo Archeologico Nazionale, 1996) Naples 1996.

S. De Caro, *Il Museo Archeologico Nazionale di Napoli. Guida alle collezioni,* Naples 1999.

S. De Caro, *Il gabinetto segreto del Museo Archeologico di Napoli*, Naples 2000.

R. Cantilena, T. Giove, *La collezione numismatica per una storia monetaria del Mezzogiorno*, Naples 2001.

M. Borriello, T. Rocco, *Il gladiatore*, Milan 2008.

*Vasi antichi. Museo Archeologico Nazionale di Napoli*, Naples 2009.

I. Bragantini, V. Sampaolo, *La pittura pompeiana*, Milan 2009.

M.P. Guidobaldi, *Ercolano. Tre secoli di scoperte*, exhibition catalogue (Naples, Museo Archeologico Nazionale, 2008-2009), Milan 2009.

*scientific coordination*
Nunzio Giustozzi

*editorial coordination*
Silvia Cassani

*graphic design*
Gianni Manna

*cover*
Tassinari/Vetta

*translation*
Joanne Berry

*photograph credits*
Archivio fotografico della
Soprintendenza Speciale per i Beni
Archeologici di Napoli e Pompei;
photographs by Luigi Spina;
Fotografica Foglia sas di Alfredo
e Pio Foglia;
Luciano Pedicini, Archivio dell'Arte

This volume was printed
by Mondadori Electa S.p.A.,
at Elcograf S.p.A.,
via Mondadori 15, Verona, in 2014